CRAC 2023 Shared Task on Multilingual Coreference Resolution

Singapore
7 December 2023

ISBN: 978-1-7138-8599-3

Printed from e-media with permission by:

Curran Associates, Inc.
57 Morehouse Lane
Red Hook, NY 12571

Some format issues inherent in the e-media version may also appear in this print version.

Printed with permission by Curran Associates, Inc. (2024)

For permission requests, please contact the Association for Computational Linguistics at the address below.

Association for Computational Linguistics
209 N. Eighth Street
Stroudsburg, Pennsylvania 18360

Phone: 1-570-476-8006
Fax: 1-570-476-0860

acl@aclweb.org

Additional copies of this publication are available from:

Curran Associates, Inc.
57 Morehouse Lane
Red Hook, NY 12571 USA
Phone: 845-758-0400
Fax: 845-758-2633
Email: curran@proceedings.com
Web: www.proceedings.com

EMNLP 2023

Proceedings of the CRAC 2023 Shared Task on Multilingual Coreference Resolution

at

The Sixth Workshop on Computational Models of Reference, Anaphora and Coreference (CRAC 2023)

CRAC 2023, an EMNLP 2023 Workshop
December 7, 2023
Singapore

Preface

This volume contains papers describing the CRAC 2023 Shared Task on Multilingual Coreference Resolution and the participating systems. The public edition of the multilingual collection CorefUD 1.1 was used as the source of training and evaluation data, spanning 17 datasets for 12 languages, namely Catalan, Czech, English, French, German, Hungarian, Lithuanian, Norwegian, Polish, Russian, Spanish, and Turkish. Shared task participants were supposed to identify mentions in texts and to predict coreference relations between the identified mentions; only identity coreference is considered in this shared task.

7 systems participated in the shared mask. In this volume, system description papers delivered by 4 teams are presented, preceded with an overview paper describing in more detail the task itself, the input data, the baseline system, the main evaluation metric, and global performance comparisons.

This year's shared task follows up on the first edition of the shared task held with CRAC 2022. The number of languages as well as the number of participating teams has grown, and we can only hope that this will become a trend.

Finally, we would like to thank all the participants for their efforts, and program committee members for reviewing the submitted manuscripts. In addition, we would like to thank all authors of the involved coreference datasets for making the results of their work publicly accessible.

November 2023
Maciej Ogrodniczuk, Zdeněk Žabokrtský
on behalf of the shared task organizers

Shared task specification

https://ufal.mff.cuni.cz/corefud/crac23

Shared task organizers

- Charles University (Prague, Czechia):
  - Anna Nedoluzhko
  - Michal Novák
  - Martin Popel
  - Zdeněk Žabokrtský
  - Daniel Zeman
- Institute of Computer Science, Polish Academy of Sciences (Warsaw, Poland):
  - Maciej Ogrodniczuk
- University of West Bohemia (Pilsen, Czechia):
  - Miloslav Konopík
  - Ondřej Pražák
  - Jakub Sido

Program Committee

- Veronique Hoste
- Miloslav Konopík
- Anna Nedoluzhko
- Vincent Ng
- Michal Novák
- Massimo Poesio
- Martin Popel
- Ondrej Prazak
- Jakub Sido
- Daniel Zeman

Invited Talk

The CRAC 2023 Shared Task on Multilingual Coreference Resolution

Milan Straka, Charles University, Czech Republic

Abstract

In a manner consistent with development in various domains of natural language processing, the performance of coreference resolution systems has been exhibiting a consistent improvement over recent years. With coreference resolution being a complex structured prediction problem, quite a few approaches have been put forth, encompassing auto-/non-autoregressive decoding, diverse mention representation, and pretrained language models of varying size and kind. In this talk, I seek to offer a review of prominent approaches and assess and compare them with a high degree of independence. Furthermore, owing to the CorefUD initiative providing datasets in many languages, I aim to empirically quantify the impact of multilingual and crosslingual transfer on the performance of the best system of the CRAC 2023 Shared Task on Multilingual Coreference Resolution.

Speaker Bio

Milan Straka is an assistant professor at the Institute of Formal and Applied Linguistics at the Faculty of Mathematics and Physics, Charles University, Prague, Czech Republic. He is the (co-)author of several shared-task-winning NLP tools like UDPipe, a morphosyntactic analyzer for currently 72 languages; PERIN, a semantic parser; and CorPipe, the winner of CRAC 2022 and 2023 shared tasks on multilingual coreference resolution. His further research interests include named entity recognition, named entity linking, grammar error correction, and multilingual models in general.

Table of Contents

Shared Task Session Program

Thursday, December 7, 2023

Welcome

9:00–9:05 *Opening and Welcome*

CRAC Shared Task Invited Talk

9:05–10:00 *Recent Computational Approaches to Coreference Resolution*
Milan Straka

CRAC Shared Task Overview

10:00–10:30 *Findings of the Second Shared Task on Multilingual Coreference Resolution*
Zdeněk Žabokrtský, Miloslav Konopík, Anna Nedoluzhko, Michal Novák, Maciej Ogrodniczuk, Martin Popel, Ondřej Pražák, Jakub Sido, Daniel Zeman and Yilun Zhu

Short Break

10:30–11:00 *Coffee Break*

CRAC Shared Task System Description Session

11:00–11:20 *Multilingual coreference resolution: Adapt and Generate*
Natalia Skachkova, Tatiana Anikina and Anna Mokhova

11:20–11:40 *Neural End-to-End Coreference Resolution using Morphological Information*
Tuğba Pamay Arslan, Kutay Acar and Gülşen Eryiğit

11:40–12:00 *ÚFAL CorPipe at CRAC 2023: Larger Context Improves Multilingual Coreference Resolution*
Milan Straka

12:00–12:20 *McGill at CRAC 2023: Multilingual Generalization of Entity-Ranking Coreference Resolution Models*
Ian Porada and Jackie Chi Kit Cheung

Closing of the Workshop

12:20–12:30 *Closing Remarks*

Findings of the Second Shared Task on Multilingual Coreference Resolution

Zdeněk Žabokrtský[1], Miloslav Konopík[2], Anna Nedoluzhko[1], Michal Novák[1], Maciej Ogrodniczuk[3], Martin Popel[1], Ondřej Pražák[2], Jakub Sido[2], Daniel Zeman[1]

[1] Charles University, Faculty of Mathematics and Physics,
Institute of Formal and Applied Linguistics, Prague, Czechia
{zabokrtsky,nedoluzko,mnovak,popel,zeman}@ufal.mff.cuni.cz

[2] University of West Bohemia, Faculty of Applied Sciences,
Department of Computer Science and Engineering, Pilsen, Czechia
konopik@kiv.zcu.cz, {ondfa,sidoj}@ntis.zcu.cz

[3] Institute of Computer Science, Polish Academy of Sciences
Warsaw, Poland, maciej.ogrodniczuk@gmail.com

Abstract

This paper summarizes the second edition of the shared task on multilingual coreference resolution, held with the CRAC 2023 workshop. Just like last year, participants of the shared task were to create trainable systems that detect mentions and group them based on identity coreference; however, this year's edition uses a slightly different primary evaluation score, and is also broader in terms of covered languages: version 1.1 of the multilingual collection of harmonized coreference resources CorefUD was used as the source of training and evaluation data this time, with 17 datasets for 12 languages. 7 systems competed in this shared task.

1 Introduction

The idea of a shared task focused on resolving coreference for multiple languages goes back to SemEval-2010 (Recasens et al., 2010) with seven languages and CoNLL-2012 (Pradhan et al., 2012) with three languages included. The amount of languages has been extended to 10 languages (with multiple datasets for some of them) in the Multilingual Coreference Resolution Shared Task at CRAC 2022 (Žabokrtský et al., 2022), making use of the CorefUD 1.0 collection (Nedoluzhko et al., 2022). This paper reports on the second edition of this shared task organized in 2023,[1] associated with CRAC again.

In brief, the most important improvements in this year's edition are the following. First, the shared task employs a newer version of the CorefUD collection. CorefUD 1.1 contains updated versions of 13 datasets (for 10 languages) already included in CorefUD 1.0, one new dataset for (already included) Hungarian, and 3 new datasets for newly added languages: 2 for Norwegian and 1 for Turkish.

Second, the original morpho-syntactic features in the development and test sets were replaced by the output of UDPipe 2 (Straka, 2018) to make the evaluation scheme more realistic (with gold feature values being available, coreference prediction might be simplified to some extent, compared to real-world application scenarios).

Third, we use the head-matching approach for mentions in the primary score in this year's edition instead of partial matching. Last year, partial matching led several teams to optimize their predicted mentions by reducing them to their syntactic heads, thereby losing the information about full mention spans.

The remainder of the paper is structured as follows. Section 2 focuses on changes of this shared task's data compared to the previous edition. Section 3 explains the evaluation metrics – the primary score as well as the supplementary ones – employed in the shared task. Section 4 describes the baseline system and the 7 participating systems. Section 5 summarizes the results. Section 6 concludes.

2 Datasets

Like the previous year, the shared task draws its training and evaluation data from the public part of

[1] https://ufal.mff.cuni.cz/corefud/crac23

Proceedings of the CRAC 2023 Shared Task on Multilingual Coreference Resolution, pages 1–18
December 7, 2023

CorefUD dataset	docs	sents	words	zeros	entities	avg. len.	non-singletons
Catalan-AnCora	1298	13,613	429,313	6,377	18,030	3.5	62,417
Czech-PCEDT	2312	49,208	1,155,755	35,844	52,721	3.3	168,138
Czech-PDT	3165	49,428	834,720	22,389	78,747	2.4	154,983
English-GUM	195	10,761	187,416	99	27,757	1.9	32,323
English-ParCorFull	19	543	10,798	0	202	4.2	835
French-Democrat	126	13,057	284,883	0	39,023	2.0	46,487
German-ParCorFull	19	543	10,602	0	259	3.5	896
German-PotsdamCC	176	2,238	33,222	0	3,752	1.4	2,519
Hungarian-KorKor	94	1,351	24,568	1,988	1,134	3.6	4,103
Hungarian-SzegedKoref	400	8,820	123,968	4,857	5,182	3.0	15,165
Lithuanian-LCC	100	1,714	37,014	0	1,224	3.7	4,337
Norwegian-BokmaalNARC	346	15,742	245,515	0	53,357	1.4	26,611
Norwegian-NynorskNARC	394	12,481	206,660	0	44,847	1.4	21,847
Polish-PCC	1828	35,874	538,885	470	127,688	1.5	82,804
Russian-RuCor	181	9,035	156,636	0	3,636	4.5	16,193
Spanish-AnCora	1356	14,159	458,418	8,112	20,115	3.5	70,663
Turkish-ITCC	24	4,733	55,341	0	690	5.3	3,668

Table 1: Data sizes in terms of the total number of documents, sentences, tokens, zeros (empty words), coreference entities, average entity length (in number of mentions) and the total number of non-singleton mentions. Train/dev/test splits of these datasets roughly follow 8/1/1 ratio. See Nedoluzhko et al. (2022) for details.

the CorefUD collection (Nedoluzhko et al., 2022),[2] now in its latest release (1.1).[3] There are 17 datasets for 12 languages (3 language families). Compared to CorefUD 1.0, which was used in the previous year of the shared task, there are 4 new datasets and 2 new languages (1 new language family): Hungarian KorKor, Norwegian NARC (Bokmål and Nynorsk versions), and Turkish ITCC.

CorefUD ensures that the datasets are unified at the file format level: They use the CoNLL-U format with extra annotation in the last column.[4] The data have not been sufficiently harmonized at the level of annotation guidelines (for example, different datasets may have different rules for the extent of a mention). Table 1 gives an overview of the datasets and their sizes.

We follow the official train/dev/test splits of CorefUD 1.1.

2.1 Updated Resources

The 13 datasets that were already available in CorefUD 1.0 are introduced in Žabokrtský et al. (2022). Instead of repeating the introduction here, we focus on changes between CorefUD 1.0 and 1.1.

[2]https://ufal.mff.cuni.cz/corefud
[3]http://hdl.handle.net/11234/1-5053
[4]https://ufal.mff.cuni.cz/~popel/corefud-1.0/corefud-1.0-format.pdf

Catalan-AnCora (ca_ancora) and **Spanish-AnCora** (es_ancora): The 3LB section of the AnCora treebank is omitted from CorefUD 1.1 because it does not contain coreference annotation. Named entities that are not annotated for coreference are omitted also in the remaining sections (previously they appeared as singletons). There are also some corrections in the LEMMA column and in dependency relations; the `arg` and `tem` semantic attributes from the original corpus are now visible in the MISC column.

Czech-PCEDT (cs_pcedt) and **Czech-PDT** (cs_pdt): Removed superfluous empty nodes (zeros) `#Rcp`, `#Cor` and `#QCor`. Removed empty nodes depending on the artificial root. Improved guessing of pronominal forms for empty nodes, fixed cases where conditional auxiliaries in multiword tokens are used to break mention spans. There are also some improvements in morphological and syntactic annotation. The tectogrammatical functors from the original corpus are now visible in the MISC column.

English-GUM (en_gum): new data from GUM v9 (published in Universal Dependencies 2.12), the total size increased from 164 to 187 thousand words.

English-ParCorFull (en_parcorfull) and **German-ParCorFull** (de_parcorfull): Morpho-syntactic annotation updated using UD 2.10 models for UDPipe 2. In addition, the conversion of the English data was fixed so that mentions are detected even in invalid files.

French-Democrat (fr_democrat): Conversion into CorefUD reimplemented, fixing multiple bugs.

German-PotsdamCC (de_potsdam), **Hungarian-SzegedKoref** (hu_szeged), **Lithuanian-LCC** (lt_lcc), **Polish-PCC** (pl_pcc), and **Russian-RuCor** (ru_rucor): Morpho-syntactic annotation updated using UD 2.10 models.

2.2 New Resources

Hungarian-KorKor (hu_korkor) (Vadász, 2022) contains texts from two sources: articles from Hungarian Wikipedia and texts from the Hungarian website of the GlobalVoices news portal. Compared to hu_szeged, the latter contains student essays and news articles. Both corpora contain zeros in subject, object, and possessor positions, but the rules for their placement are not identical. Moreover, the tagset of coreference and anaphora relations are different as well.

Norwegian-BokmaalNARC and **Norwegian-NynorskNARC** (no_bokmaalnarc, no_nynorsknarc) (Mæhlum et al., 2022) are based on parts of the Norwegian Dependency Treebank (NDT), which contains mostly news texts, but also government reports, parliamentary transcripts, and blogs in the two varieties of written Norwegian – Bokmål and Nynorsk. Train/dev/test splits correspond to those in the UD version of the NDT treebank.

Turkish-ITCC (tr_itcc) (Pamay and Eryiğit, 2018) is based on the Marmara Turkish Coreference Corpus, which in turn contains documents from the METU Turkish Corpus. There is an overlap between ITCC and the UD Turkish IMST treebank. The gold-standard morphosyntactic annotation of sentences that occur in both datasets was taken from IMST; the remaining sentences were parsed by a model trained on IMST. Train/dev/test split in the shared task follows that of CorefUD.[5] The coreference annotation in this corpus is less advanced than in the other corpora in CorefUD: some paragraphs completely lack coreference annotation, in some other paragraphs coreference is annotated only partially. Annotation of zeros is missing in the current version.

2.3 Data pre-processing

For training and tuning purposes, we have provided the participants with the train and dev sets as they were released in CorefUD 1.1, i.e. with gold coreference annotation for all datasets and manually annotated morpho-syntactic features for the datasets that originally include them. However, in the dev and test sets intended for evaluation (and submitting), we have deleted the corefence annotation and replaced original morpho-syntax features by the outputs of UD 2.10 models for all datasets, even those in which these features were originally human-annotated. Although it makes the evaluation setup more realistic, there is still room for improvement as this has not affected zeros. Similarly to last year's edition, participants have been given the input documents with zeros already reconstructed.

3 Evaluation Metrics

Systems participating in the shared task are evaluated with the CorefUD scorer.[6] The primary evaluation score is the CoNLL F_1 score with singletons excluded and using *head* mention matching, which is a change to the last year's edition, where *partial* mention matching was used in the primary score. In addition, we calculate several other supplementary scores to compare the shared task submissions.

Official scorer We use the CorefUD scorer to evaluate participants' submissions. It is built on the Universal Anaphora (UA) scorer 1.0 (Yu et al., 2022)[7] taking advantage of the implementations of all generally used coreferential measures with no modifications. Additionally, the CorefUD scorer introduces the implementation of head match and the Mention Overlap Ratio (MOR; Žabokrtský et al., 2022). It also supports matching of potentially discontinuous mentions and anaphor-level evaluation of zeros. Naturally, it is also compatible with the CorefUD 1.0 file format.[8]

[5]The CorefUD ITCC data split is not compatible with the IMST treebank data split in Universal Dependencies 2.12 because the sentences were shuffled in IMST. An improved version of IMST is prepared for UD 2.13 to be released in November 2023: The original ordering of sentences from METU is restored, sentence identifiers refer to METU, document boundaries are marked and data split is made compatible with ITCC.

[6]https://github.com/ufal/corefud-scorer

[7]This in turn reimplements the official CoNLL-2012 scorer (Pradhan et al., 2014).

[8]After the scorer for the shared task had been frozen, the UA scorer 2.0 (Yu et al., 2023), which integrates most of the new features from the CorefUD scorer, was released as a result of the cooperation of the authors of the two scorers.

Mention matching Within the CorefUD collection, some datasets do not specify mention spans in their original annotations (e.g. cs_pdt, hu_korkor). In such datasets, a mention is primarily identified by its head and loosely associated with a dependency subtree rooted in this head. Additionally, in other datasets, it can be challenging to precisely define mention boundaries, particularly when mentions involve embedded clauses, long detailed specifications, etc. On the other hand, some of the original sources from CorefUD do not annotate mention heads at all (e.g. de_potsdam, lt_lcc). Consequently, CorefUD addresses this issue by specifying both the mention span and its head for each mention in all its datasets. While mention spans are derived using the dependency tree only if they are not present in the original source, mention heads are always determined from the tree[9] using the Udapi block `corefud.MoveHead`.[10]

The availability of both spans and heads in gold annotation allows for various possible ways of mention matching in the evaluation. Last year, the participants were asked to predict only the span boundaries in order to keep the task simple. To compensate for the drawbacks of *exact matching* (i.e., precise matching of the full span), we proposed the *partial mention matching* method and used it also in the primary score. A partial match of a predicted mention to a gold mention is found if all its words are included in the gold mention and one of them is the gold head. Nevertheless, this approach appeared to be problematic. It encouraged some participants to post-process their predictions by reducing the full mention spans to the head word only. First, since not all the participants applied this post-processing, it made the comparison of the participants' submissions slightly unfair. To rectify this imbalance, we evaluated the submissions also with a head match, deriving the mention heads automatically using the same method as for the gold spans. More importantly, forced shrinkage of predicted mention spans performed by some of the teams resulted in loss of the original mention spans produced by their systems. Consequently, such submissions failed in the evaluation with the exact match.

For this year's edition, we decided to use *head match* in the primary metric. Two mentions are considered matching if their heads correspond to identical tokens. If there are multiple gold or predicted mentions with the same head, full spans are taken into account but only to disambiguate between multiple mentions with the same head. Otherwise, full mention spans are ignored.

Therefore, the participants were expected to predict mention heads in their submissions. However, due to the disambiguation rules we encouraged the participants to predict the mention span boundaries as well. In addition, their presence allows us to evaluate the systems with respect to exact matching as one of the supplementary scores.

Note that the participants were also free to use the Udapi block `corefud.MoveHead` in order to derive the mention head from the dependency tree, if their systems were not able to predict the heads by their own means.[11]

Singletons New additions to the CorefUD collection have not altered the dominance of the datasets without the annotation of singletons, i.e., entities comprising only a single mention. We thus keep the setup from the last year's edition and calculate the primary score excluding potential singletons in both gold and predicted coreference chains.

Primary score As is usual for coreference resolution tasks, we employed the CoNLL F_1 score (Denis and Baldridge, 2009; Pradhan et al., 2014) as the primary evaluation score. It is an unweighted average of the F_1 scores of three coreference metrics: MUC (Vilain et al., 1995), B^3 (Bagga and Baldwin, 1998) and CEAF-e (Luo, 2005), each adopting a different view on coreference relations, namely link-based, mention-based and entity-based, respectively. A single primary score providing a final ranking of participating submissions is a macro-average over all datasets in the CorefUD test collection.

Supplementary scores In addition to the primary CoNLL F_1 score, we calculate alternative versions of this metric using different ways of mention matching: partial-match and exact-match. Note

[9] Note that some datasets label a semantic head (single word) or a minimal span (multiple words possible, e.g. in ARRAU, Uryupina et al., 2020), i.e., a unit that carries the most crucial semantic information, instead. Nedoluzhko et al. (2021) have shown though that heads labeled in coreference annotation most often correspond to heads in a dependency tree.

[10] `https://github.com/udapi/udapi-python/blob/master/udapi/block/corefud/movehead.py`

[11] All of the participants used this Udapi block for predicting heads (or another method with identical results on the test set).

that the partial-match setup was used as the primary score in the last year's edition. Furthermore, we compute the primary metrics using the head-match for all mentions including singletons.

Besides the primary score, we also report the systems' performance in terms of the coreference measures that contribute to the CoNLL score as well as other standard measures, e.g. BLANC (Recasens and Hovy, 2011) and LEA (Moosavi and Strube, 2016). To evaluate the quality of mention matching while ignoring the assignment of mentions to coreferential entities, we use the MOR score. Last but not least, we also measure the performance of the systems on zeros using the anaphor-decomposable score for zeros (Žabokrtský et al., 2022), which is an application of the scoring schema proposed by Tuggener (2014).

4 Participating Systems

4.1 Baseline

Same as last year, the baseline system is the end-to-end neural coreference resolution system based on Pražák et al. (2021).[12] The model solves both tasks (mention prediction and coreference linking) at the same time. It goes through all the possible mention spans and learns to predict the antecedent of each span. In case a span is not the correct mention or it is the singleton the model learns to align it to the artificial antecedent. Therefore, the model is not able to predict singletons. During training, the marginal probability of all the correct antecedents of each mention is maximized. More details can be found in Pražák et al. (2021).

4.2 System Submissions

This year, 7 teams participated in the shared task. The descriptions below are based on the information provided by the respective participants in an online questionnaire. As the authors of the DeepBlueAI system have neither provided us with any details nor submitted their system description paper, we cannot include it among the descriptions.

Anonymous[13] The system initially drew inspiration from wl-coref (Dobrovolskii, 2021), accounting for head information. The authors found that XLM-Roberta yields the best results, leading to its selection for subsequent tests. They developed a conversion system to manage the CoNLL-U format as jsonlines. Furthermore, they efficiently incorporate new features (e.g., UPOS, DEPREL, FEATS) with Udapi assistance. Alongside the CoNLL features, a BIO-like scheme is added to the indices in mention spans. Various distance/matching features and context sizes are used to update token scores for potential antecedents. The results primarily depend on a model's ability to construct the assigned scheme, where the head (B) is the primary focus of this specific task. Future work plans include leveraging similarity- and classification properties through fine-tuning sentence embeddings to further enhance span detection and merging. The authors note that they did not conduct any ablation study, and there is still much to explore regarding the usefulness of features.

CorPipe[14] ÚFAL CorPipe is a minor evolution from the system implemented in the previous year (Straka and Straková, 2022). All models undergo training on the concatenation of all treebanks. They utilize either the mT5-large pre-trained model or the mT5-xl pre-trained model. The architecture remains the same, with a few modifications: The system employs 2560 subwords during prediction, which is possible due to the relative embeddings in mT5. Instead of using CRF to perform mention span detection (since it would be complicated to ensemble), the authors train the model using standard classification into generalized BIO encoding, allowing overlapping mentions. Subsequently, a dynamic programming algorithm performs structured prediction, whose output always presents a valid sequence of BIO tags. Ensembling takes place during both the mention span detection and the coreference linking. The ÚFAL CorPipe team submits multiple configurations – one best-performing mT5-large-sized model, one best-performing mT5-xl-sized model, a best-performing checkpoint selected for each treebank independently, and the best submission that is an ensemble of 3 checkpoints chosen for each treebank independently. See Straka (2023) in this volume for details.

DFKI-Adapt[15] The DFKI-Adapt system is based on the baseline system provided by the organizers. This system augments it by adding character embeddings for each token to the original input

[12] https://github.com/ondfa/coref-multiling

[13] The authors of this system asked us to anonymize this submission.

[14] The CorPipe system was submitted to CodaLab by user "straka" from team ÚFAL CorPipe.

[15] The DFKI-Adapt system was submitted to CodaLab by user "tatiana.anikina" from team DFKI_TR.

embeddings (based on multilingual BERT) using LSTM (300 dimensions). The training procedure starts with pre-training the joint model utilizing all languages combined into a single training set. Following this step, the team merges the datasets for the related languages (for example, all Slavic or Romance languages) and fine-tunes a separate model for each language using these combined datasets. Additionally, they train the language-specific task adapters added to the BERT model. During the training process, they sort all documents after every epoch according to their difficulty for the model, as determined by the loss function. The most challenging instances are chosen for further model finetuning before the next epoch begins. The DFKI-Adapt system employs no external resources for training, relying solely on the Shared Task data.

DFKI-MPrompt[16] The DFKI-MPrompt system integrates two independent modules. One module performs mention generation based on prompt learning facilitated by the OpenPrompt library. Using a prefix template and a frozen mT5-large model, the prompt model generates all possible mentions within a given sentence, including their indices. The training of this single prompt model encompasses all languages. The other module uses the baseline trained on gold mentions. Given the availability of gold mentions, the baseline's mention scorer is not utilized. The baseline also undergoes training on the combined datasets. In the final stage, the authors input the mentions generated by the prompt model to the baseline to identify coreferent pairs.

McGill[17] The McGill system is based on the Longdoc "unbounded memory" model (Toshniwal et al., 2020). It is similar to end-to-end coreference (Lee et al., 2017) adapted for BERT (Joshi et al., 2019). The primary difference is that the model has a discrete set of candidate entities. The McGill system uses the same hyperparameters that Toshniwal et al. (2021) use for the PreCo dataset, with the following exceptions: Speaker information is included at the start of each sentence if present in the dataset. A language embedding is defined for each dataset using the same configuration as the genre embedding used by Lee et al. (2017). The McGill model uses a batch size of 1, similar to most other models based on Lee et al. (2017). The authors experimented with using XLM-Roberta (Conneau et al., 2020) and mT5 (Xue et al., 2021) *Large* model sizes as the language model encoder. They found that XLM-Roberta leads to better performance, so they used XLM-Roberta Large in the final submission. The McGill team trained the model for 60k steps. In the first 50k steps, they trained their model on all datasets weighted by the number of documents in the dataset. For the last 10k steps, they trained the model on all datasets weighted equally. The model with the best performance on the development set, corresponding to 57.5k steps, was submitted. The McGill model predicts only coreferring spans. Therefore, the McGill team estimated mention heads using Udapi following the same method as the shared-task baseline. For details, see Porada and Cheung (2023) in this volume.

Morfbase[18] The Morfbase system enhances the baseline system by incorporating morphological features, drawing inspiration from Pamay Arslan and Eryiğit (2023). These linguistic features, represented as one-hot vectors, are concatenated to BERT representations. Both the mention detection and coreference linking stages utilize these hand-crafted linguistic features. The team used the provided heuristic head detection script on the model outputs to estimate the heads of the predicted mentions. The primary goal of this model is to enhance coreference performance, particularly for pro-dropped and morphologically rich languages. See Pamay Arslan et al. (2023) in this volume for details.

Ondfa The UWB system remains identical to the one submitted in the previous year, optimized for the new metric (Pražák and Konopík, 2022). It builds on the baseline system with several modifications. Initially, the team trains a joint cross-lingual model (XLMR-large) for all datasets. Subsequently, they fine-tune this model for each dataset separately. The model learns to predict the heads of the mentions from the original spans. They either use head prediction or whole span prediction with `corefud.MoveHead` (chosen for each dataset separately based on the performance on the dev dataset). Syntax trees are also incorporated as features into the model. Additionally, the UWB team modified the model to handle singletons.

[16]The DFKI-MPrompt system was submitted to CodaLab by user "natalia_s" from team DFKI_TR.

[17]The McGill system was submitted to CodaLab by user "ianpo".

[18]The Morfbase system was submitted to CodaLab by user "TugbaP" from team TrCR, originally under the name "itunlp".

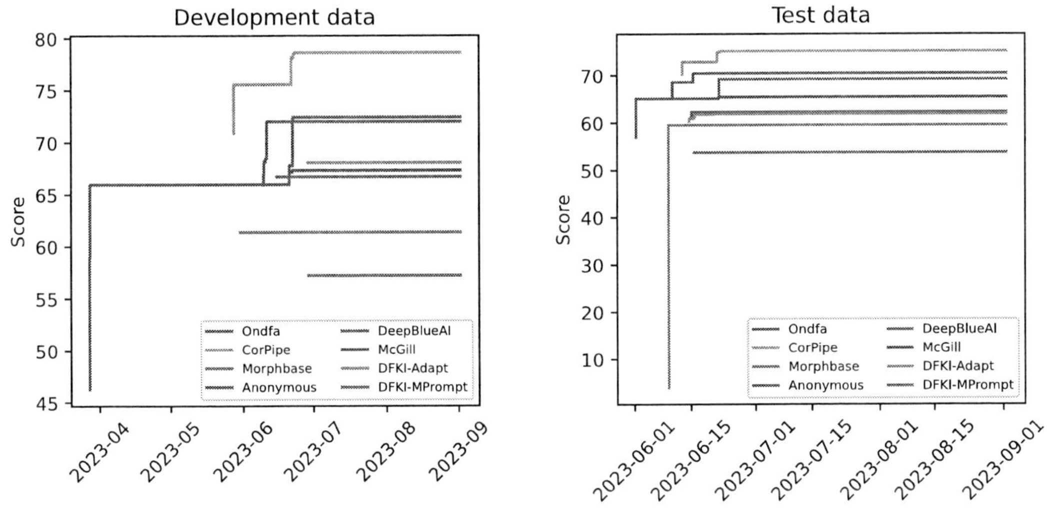

Figure 1: The evolution of the competition in the development (left) and the test phase (right).

4.3 System Comparison

Table 2 shows the basic properties of all submitted systems for evaluation. Half of the submissions based their systems on the provided baseline. The participants who used the baseline model either used it as it is, or added some modifications to it, such as soft prompt, tuning per language, or changing the sequence length.

Comparing Tables 2 and 3 reveals that results generally improve with larger model sizes, apart from some exceptions. This is expected, as larger models have more parameters and can capture more information and nuances from the data. However, larger models also require more computational resources and time to train and run, which could be a challenge for some participants.

5 Results and Comparison

5.1 Evolution of CodaLab Submissions

Across the two phases of the competition, participants had access to the official evaluation scripts, enabling them to track and evaluate the metrics dynamically. We also encouraged them to send continuous results into the CodaLab system.[19] After the competition, we collected all continuously received results from all contributors. The competition evolved as participants refined their models and strategies. We can see non-negligible progress in Figure 1 in terms of observed metrics during both phases, which was caused most probably by competition among participants, who could check the results of others during all phases.

5.2 Main Results

The main results are summarized in Table 3. The CorPipe system is the best one according to the official primary metric (head-match excluding singletons) as well as according to three alternative metrics: partial-match excluding singletons (which was the primary metric last year), exact-match excluding singletons and head-match including singletons. The Anonymous system is the second best according to all four metrics. All metrics result in the same ordering of systems with a single exception of the Ondfa system, which is the second worst according to exact-match, but the third best according to other metrics. This is caused by the fact that for some datasets (cf. description of Ondfa in Section 4.2), Ondfa predicted only the head word and the span was always just this single word.

Table 4 shows recall, precision, and F1 for six metrics. The F1 scores of the first five metrics (MUC. B^3, BLANC, and LEA) result in exactly the same ordering of systems (same as the primary metric). Most of the systems have higher precision than recall for all the metrics, but the highest disbalance is in the BASELINE system. CorPipe is the only system that has higher recall than precision for at least some metrics (MUC and CEAF-e), but other metrics have similar precision and recall.

The MOR metric (mention overlap ratio) mea-

[19] `https://codalab.lisn.upsaclay.fr/competitions/11800`

Name	Baseline?	Pretrained model	Model size	Seq. length
Anonymous	No	xlm-roberta-base	1-20M (various)	512
BASELINE	Yes	bert-base	220M	512
CorPipe	No	google/mt5-large, google/mt5-xl	567M, 1.7G (two sizes)	512, 2560
DFKI-Adapt	Yes	bert-base	259M	512
DFKI-MPrompt	Yes	bert-base + soft prompt	221M	512
McGill	No	xlm-roberta-large	596M	512
Morfbase	Yes	bert-base	219M	512
Ondfa	Yes	xlm-roberta-large	600M	512

Name	Tuned per lang.?	Batch size	Tuned hyperparameters
Anonymous	Some (l. families)	16	2 – Input size, learning rate
BASELINE	No	1 doc	0
CorPipe	No	8, 12, 16, 32	4 – Model size, batch size, learning rate, epochs
DFKI-Adapt	Yes	1 doc	3 – Dropout, mention loss coef, task LR
DFKI-MPrompt	No	1 sent + 1 doc	0
McGill	No	1	1 – Number of training steps
Morfbase	No	256	0
Ondfa	Yes	1 doc	4 – Specific for the model

Table 2: The table compares properties of systems participating in the task (except for the DeepBlueAI system, as there are no details available) . The systems are ordered alphabetically. The shortcuts in headings are defined as follows: **Name** is the name of the submission, **Baseline?** indicates whether they used a baseline model or not, **Tuned per lang.?** indicates whether they tuned their model for each language or not. **various** in Anonymous means various settings depending on features and architecture.

sures only the mention matching quality, while ignoring the coreference, but even then the ordering of systems is similar to the primary metric (Ondfa is the third worst according to MOR, again because it does not predict full spans for some datasets).

Table 5 shows that the CorPipe system consistently outperforms the other submissions across all datasets and languages. Furthermore, the low results on tr_itcc confirm that the annotation of coreference is unfinished in this dataset. Similarly, we experienced an unexpectedly low performance of submissions on en_parcorfull in the 2022 edition of the shared task. This was a consequence of the small size of the dataset and an error in the CorefUD conversion pipeline, making one of the two documents in the test set completely missing all coreference annotation. The error was fixed this year, but the English and German ParCorFull datasets remain the smallest ones in CorefUD, so there is a high risk of overfitting. We admit such outliers may have a negative impact on the overall score, especially if macro-averaging is used in the primary score to weigh performance on individual datasets. However, we still believe that due to differences in languages and annotation standards, each dataset should contribute equally. The impact of potential errors in some datasets is then mitigated by the number of contributing datasets.

5.3 Evaluation of Zeros

Table 6 focuses on the evaluation of zero anaphors for individual languages where anaphoric zeros are annotated.[20] The F1 scores are again highly correlated with the primary score, with the exception of pl_pcc, where CorPipe was outperformed by Ondfa (4 points better) and DeepBleuAI (1 point better). However, according to Table 1, pl_pcc has a very small number of zeros annotated, so these results are not reliable.

5.4 Further analysis

Similarly to last year, we provide several additional tables in the appendices to shed more light on the differences between the submitted systems.

Tables 7–8 show results factorized according to the different universal part of speech tags (UPOS) in the mention heads. Table 7 contains results on datasets where all entities without any mention with a given UPOS as head were deleted. Table 8 contains results on datasets where all mentions without a given UPOS as head were deleted, so these results may be a bit misleading because e.g. the PRON

[20] Recall that the setup for zeros is slightly unrealistic (see Section 2.3).

system	excluding singletons			with singletons
	head-match	**partial-match**	**exact-match**	**head-match**
CorPipe	**74.90**	**73.33** (-1.57)	**71.46** (-3.44)	**76.82** (+1.91)
Anonymous	70.41	69.23 (-1.18)	67.09 (-3.32)	73.20 (+2.79)
Ondfa	69.19	68.93 (-0.26)	53.01 (-16.18)	68.37 (-0.82)
McGill	65.43	64.56 (-0.88)	63.13 (-2.30)	68.23 (+2.80)
DeepBlueAI	62.29	61.32 (-0.98)	59.95 (-2.34)	54.51 (-7.78)
DFKI-Adapt	61.86	60.83 (-1.03)	59.18 (-2.69)	53.94 (-7.92)
Morfbase	59.53	58.49 (-1.05)	56.89 (-2.64)	52.07 (-7.47)
BASELINE	56.96	56.28 (-0.68)	54.75 (-2.21)	49.32 (-7.64)
DFKI-MPrompt	53.76	51.62 (-2.15)	50.42 (-3.35)	46.83 (-6.93)

Table 3: Main results: the CoNLL metric macro-averaged over all datasets. The table shows the primary metric (head-match excluding singletons) and three alternative metrics: partial-match excluding singletons, exact-match excluding singletons and head-match with singletons. A difference relative to the primary metric is reported in parenthesis. The best score in each column is in bold. The systems are ordered by the primary metric.

system	MUC	B^3	CEAF-e	BLANC	LEA	MOR
CorPipe	**80 / 79 / 80**	**73 / 73 / 73**	**73 / 71 / 72**	**72 / 73 / 72**	**70 / 71 / 70**	**79** / 80 / **79**
Anonymous	74 / 78 / 76	65 / 72 / 68	67 / 68 / 67	63 / 71 / 66	62 / 69 / 65	74 / 78 / 76
Ondfa	74 / 78 / 75	64 / 71 / 67	64 / 67 / 66	62 / 70 / 65	61 / 68 / 64	52 / 83 / 63
McGill	69 / 76 / 71	60 / 69 / 63	58 / 68 / 62	58 / 68 / 61	57 / 66 / 60	59 / 82 / 67
DeepBlueAI	67 / 74 / 70	56 / 65 / 59	55 / 63 / 58	53 / 64 / 56	53 / 61 / 56	61 / 81 / 67
DFKI-Adapt	66 / 73 / 69	56 / 65 / 59	56 / 62 / 58	53 / 63 / 56	52 / 61 / 55	58 / 80 / 66
Morfbase	63 / 71 / 66	51 / 65 / 56	56 / 58 / 56	47 / 62 / 52	47 / 61 / 52	59 / 78 / 66
BASELINE	56 / 76 / 63	46 / 69 / 54	48 / 62 / 54	44 / 67 / 51	42 / 64 / 49	49 / **87** / 61
DFKI-MPrompt	57 / 67 / 61	45 / 60 / 50	49 / 56 / 51	41 / 57 / 45	40 / 55 / 45	57 / 71 / 62

Table 4: Recall / Precision / F1 for individual secondary metrics. All scores macro-averaged over all datasets.

system	ca_ancora	cs_pcedt	cs_pdt	de_parcorfull	de_potsdam	en_gum	en_parcorfull	es_ancora	fr_democrat	hu_korkor	hu_szeged	lt_lcc	no_bokmaalnarc	no_nynorsknarc	pl_pcc	ru_rucor	tr_itcc
CorPipe	**82.59**	**79.33**	**79.20**	**72.12**	**71.09**	**76.57**	**69.86**	**83.39**	**69.82**	**68.92**	**69.47**	**75.87**	**78.74**	**78.77**	**79.54**	**82.46**	**55.63**
Anonymous	79.51	75.88	76.39	64.37	68.24	72.29	59.02	80.52	66.13	64.65	66.25	70.09	75.32	73.33	77.58	80.19	47.22
Ondfa	76.02	74.82	74.67	71.86	69.37	71.56	61.62	77.18	60.32	66.38	65.75	68.52	72.39	70.91	76.90	76.50	41.52
McGill	71.75	67.67	70.88	41.58	70.20	66.72	47.27	73.78	65.17	60.74	65.93	65.77	73.73	72.43	76.14	77.28	45.28
DeepBlueAI	67.55	70.38	69.93	48.81	63.90	63.58	43.33	69.52	55.69	54.38	63.14	66.75	69.86	68.53	73.11	74.41	36.14
DFKI-Adapt	68.21	68.72	67.34	52.52	69.28	65.11	36.87	69.19	58.96	51.53	58.56	66.01	70.05	68.21	67.98	72.48	40.67
Morfbase	68.23	64.89	64.74	39.96	64.87	62.80	40.81	69.01	53.18	52.91	56.41	64.08	68.17	66.35	67.88	68.53	39.22
BASELINE	65.26	67.72	65.22	44.11	57.13	63.08	35.19	66.93	55.31	40.71	55.32	63.57	65.10	65.78	66.08	69.03	22.75
DFKI-MPrompt	55.45	60.39	56.13	40.34	59.75	57.83	34.32	58.31	52.96	44.53	48.79	56.52	65.12	62.99	61.15	61.96	37.44

Table 5: Results for individual languages in the primary metric (CoNLL).

system	ca_ancora	cs_pdt	cs_pcedt	es_ancora	hu_korkor	hu_szeged	pl_pcc
CorPipe	**93 / 92 / 92**	**91 / 92 / 92**	**87 / 88 / 87**	**94** / 95 / **95**	**82** / 89 / **85**	**88** / 70 / 78	75 / 69 / 72
Anonymous	91 / 90 / 91	90 / 91 / 90	86 / 86 / 86	94 / 95 / 94	79 / **89** / 84	83 / **74** / 78	71 / 63 / 67
Ondfa	91 / 90 / 91	90 / 92 / 91	86 / 87 / 87	**94** / 94 / 94	77 / 87 / 82	86 / 74 / **79**	**79** / 73 / **76**
McGill	89 / 90 / 89	88 / 89 / 89	82 / 87 / 84	92 / **95** / 94	81 / 85 / 83	81 / 73 / 77	71 / 65 / 68
DeepBlueAI	85 / 89 / 87	86 / 90 / 88	83 / 86 / 85	91 / 94 / 93	75 / 79 / 77	78 / 70 / 74	**79** / 68 / 73
DFKI-Adapt	85 / 84 / 84	84 / 85 / 84	78 / 81 / 80	89 / 89 / 89	67 / 77 / 72	67 / 61 / 64	62 / 68 / 65
Morfbase	84 / 85 / 85	81 / 84 / 83	78 / 81 / 80	88 / 89 / 88	57 / 73 / 64	61 / 57 / 59	33 / 40 / 36
BASELINE	82 / 82 / 82	81 / 84 / 82	77 / 81 / 79	87 / 88 / 87	60 / 68 / 64	61 / 57 / 59	50 / **80** / 62
DFKI-MPrompt	78 / 83 / 80	78 / 85 / 81	72 / 79 / 75	78 / 87 / 82	69 / 70 / 69	59 / 45 / 51	46 / 55 / 50

Table 6: Recall / Precision / F1 for anaphor-decomposable score of coreference resolution on zero anaphors across individual languages. Only the datasets that contain anaphoric zeros are listed (en_gum excluded as all zeros in its test set are non-anaphoric). Note that these scores are directly comparable to neither the CoNLL score nor to the supplementary scores calculated with respect to whole entities in Table 4.

column does not consider all pronominal coreference, but only pronoun-to-pronoun coreference. An entity with one pronoun and one noun mention is excluded from this table (because it becomes a singleton after deleting noun or pronoun mentions and singletons are excluded from the evaluation in these tables).

Tables 9–12 show various statistics on the entities and mentions in a concatenation of all the test sets. Note that such statistics are mostly influenced by larger datasets. Tables 13–16 show the same statistics for cs_pcedt, which is the largest dataset in CorefUD 1.1 (as for the number of words and non-singleton mentions).

6 Conclusions and Future Work

Both editions of the shared task attracted a substantial number of participants and led to an increase in the state of the art. Hence, the success of the two completed shared tasks supports us in the idea of continuing this initiative in the future.

However, there are challenges, too. For instance, the underlying data collection is still somewhat limited from the typological perspective, and thus our ambition is to add more languages with substantially different typological structures, experiment with other writing systems, or add a historical perspective with data from classical languages.

There are also more technical questions that would deserve a discussion in the future, such as whether weightless macro-averaging is the best approach for data collections with order-of-magnitude differences in training and testing data sizes. Similarly, substantial differences in internal annotation consistency in individual resources is also an issue from the evaluation viewpoint, since, for example, optimizing performance for a low-quality resource might lead to substantial performance gains, which, however, may correspond to systematic deficiencies present in the data rather than objective quality.

Finally, we aim to progress to a fully realistic evaluation setup which starts from raw or pre-tokenized text. Participants would be then expected to reconstruct zeros.

Acknowledgements

This work was supported by the Grant 20-16819X (LUSyD) of the Czech Science Foundation (GAČR); LM2023062 (LINDAT/CLARIAH-CZ) of the Ministry of Education, Youth, and Sports of the Czech Republic; FW03010656 of the Technology Agency of the Czech Republic; the European Regional Development Fund as a part of 2014–2020 Smart Growth Operational Programme, CLARIN — Common Language Resources and Technology Infrastructure, project no. POIR.04.02.00-00C002/19; the project co-financed by the Polish Ministry of Education and Science under the agreement 2022/WK/09; and SGS-2022-016 Advanced methods of data processing and analysis. We thank all the participants of the shared task for participating and for providing brief descriptions of their systems. We also thank anonymous reviewers for very useful remarks.

References

Amit Bagga and Breck Baldwin. 1998. Algorithms for scoring coreference chains. In *Proceedings of The First International Conference on Language Resources and Evaluation Workshop on Linguistics Coreference*, pages 563–566.

Peter Bourgonje and Manfred Stede. 2020. The Potsdam Commentary Corpus 2.2: Extending Annotations for Shallow Discourse Parsing. In *Proceedings of the 12th Language Resources and Evaluation Conference*, pages 1061–1066, Marseille, France. European Language Resources Association.

Alexis Conneau, Kartikay Khandelwal, Naman Goyal, Vishrav Chaudhary, Guillaume Wenzek, Francisco Guzmán, Edouard Grave, Myle Ott, Luke Zettlemoyer, and Veselin Stoyanov. 2020. Unsupervised cross-lingual representation learning at scale. In *Proceedings of the 58th Annual Meeting of the Association for Computational Linguistics*, pages 8440–8451, Online. Association for Computational Linguistics.

Pascal Denis and Jason Baldridge. 2009. Global joint models for coreference resolution and named entity classification. *Procesamiento del Lenguaje Natural*, (42):87–96.

Vladimir Dobrovolskii. 2021. Word-level coreference resolution. In *Proceedings of the 2021 Conference on Empirical Methods in Natural Language Processing*, pages 7670–7675, Online and Punta Cana, Dominican Republic. Association for Computational Linguistics.

Jan Hajič, Eduard Bejček, Jaroslava Hlaváčová, Marie Mikulová, Milan Straka, Jan Štěpánek, and Barbora Štěpánková. 2020. Prague Dependency Treebank - Consolidated 1.0. In *Proceedings of the 12th International Conference on Language Resources and Evaluation (LREC 2020)*, pages 5208–5218, Marseille, France. European Language Resources Association.

Mandar Joshi, Omer Levy, Luke Zettlemoyer, and Daniel Weld. 2019. BERT for coreference resolution: Baselines and analysis. In *Proceedings of the 2019 Conference on Empirical Methods in Natural Language Processing and the 9th International Joint Conference on Natural Language Processing (EMNLP-IJCNLP)*, pages 5803–5808, Hong Kong, China. Association for Computational Linguistics.

Frédéric Landragin. 2021. Le corpus Democrat et son exploitation. Présentation. *Langages*, 224:11–24.

Ekaterina Lapshinova-Koltunski, Christian Hardmeier, and Pauline Krielke. 2018. ParCorFull: a Parallel Corpus Annotated with Full Coreference. In *Proceedings of the Eleventh International Conference on Language Resources and Evaluation (LREC 2018)*, Miyazaki, Japan. European Language Resources Association.

Kenton Lee, Luheng He, Mike Lewis, and Luke Zettlemoyer. 2017. End-to-end neural coreference resolution. In *Proceedings of the 2017 Conference on Empirical Methods in Natural Language Processing*, pages 188–197, Copenhagen, Denmark. Association for Computational Linguistics.

Xiaoqiang Luo. 2005. On coreference resolution performance metrics. In *Proceedings of the Conference on Human Language Technology and Empirical Methods in Natural Language Processing*, HLT 2005, pages 25–32. Association for Computational Linguistics.

Petter Mæhlum, Dag Haug, Tollef Jørgensen, Andre Kåsen, Anders Nøklestad, Egil Rønningstad, Per Erik Solberg, Erik Velldal, and Lilja Øvrelid. 2022. NARC–Norwegian anaphora resolution corpus. In *Proceedings of the Fifth Workshop on Computational Models of Reference, Anaphora and Coreference*, pages 48–60, Gyeongju, Korea. Association for Computational Linguistics.

Nafise Sadat Moosavi and Michael Strube. 2016. Which coreference evaluation metric do you trust? a proposal for a link-based entity aware metric. In *Proceedings of the 54th Annual Meeting of the Association for Computational Linguistics (Volume 1: Long Papers)*, pages 632–642, Berlin, Germany. Association for Computational Linguistics.

Anna Nedoluzhko, Michal Novák, Silvie Cinková, Marie Mikulová, and Jiří Mírovský. 2016. Coreference in Prague Czech-English Dependency Treebank. In *Proceedings of the Tenth International Conference on Language Resources and Evaluation (LREC 2016)*, pages 169–176, Portorož, Slovenia. European Language Resources Association.

Anna Nedoluzhko, Michal Novák, Martin Popel, Zdeněk Žabokrtský, Amir Zeldes, and Daniel Zeman. 2022. CorefUD 1.0: Coreference meets Universal Dependencies. In *Proceedings of the Thirteenth Language Resources and Evaluation Conference*, pages 4859–4872, Marseille, France. European Language Resources Association.

Anna Nedoluzhko, Michal Novák, Martin Popel, Zdeněk Žabokrtský, and Daniel Zeman. 2021. Is one head enough? Mention heads in coreference annotations compared with UD-style heads. In *Proceedings of the Sixth International Conference on Dependency Linguistics (Depling, SyntaxFest 2021)*, pages 101–114, Stroudsburg, PA, USA. Association for Computational Linguistics.

Maciej Ogrodniczuk, Katarzyna Glowińska, Mateusz Kopeć, Agata Savary, and Magdalena Zawisławska. 2013. Polish Coreference Corpus. In *Human Language Technology. Challenges for Computer Science and Linguistics — 6th Language and Technology Conference (LTC 2013), Revised Selected Papers*, volume 9561 of *Lecture Notes in Computer Science*, pages 215–226. Springer.

Maciej Ogrodniczuk, Katarzyna Głowińska, Mateusz Kopeć, Agata Savary, and Magdalena Zawisławska. 2015. *Coreference in Polish: Annotation, Resolution and Evaluation*. Walter De Gruyter.

Tuğba Pamay and Gülşen Eryiğit. 2018. Turkish Coreference Resolution. In *2018 Innovations in Intelligent Systems and Applications (INISTA)*, pages 1–7.

Tuğba Pamay Arslan, Kutay Acar, and Gülşen Eryiğit. 2023. Neural End-to-End Coreference Resolution using Morphological Information. In *Proceedings of the CRAC 2023 Shared Task on Multilingual Coreference Resolution*, pages 34–40.

Tuğba Pamay Arslan and Gülşen Eryiğit. 2023. Incorporating Dropped Pronouns into Coreference Resolution: The case for Turkish. In *Proceedings of the 17th Conference of the European Chapter of the Association for Computational Linguistics: Student Research Workshop*, pages 14–25.

Ian Porada and Jackie Chi Kit Cheung. 2023. McGill at CRAC 2023: Multilingual Generalization of Entity-Ranking Coreference Resolution Models. In *Proceedings of the CRAC 2023 Shared Task on Multilingual Coreference Resolution*, pages 52–57.

Sameer Pradhan, Xiaoqiang Luo, Marta Recasens, Eduard Hovy, Vincent Ng, and Michael Strube. 2014. Scoring Coreference Partitions of Predicted Mentions: A Reference Implementation. In *Proceedings of the 52nd Annual Meeting of the Association for Computational Linguistics (Volume 2: Short Papers)*, pages 30–35, Baltimore, Maryland. Association for Computational Linguistics.

Sameer Pradhan, Alessandro Moschitti, Nianwen Xue, Olga Uryupina, and Yuchen Zhang. 2012. CoNLL-2012 Shared Task: Modeling Multilingual Unrestricted Coreference in OntoNotes. In *Joint Conference on EMNLP and CoNLL - Shared Task*, pages 1–40, Jeju Island, Korea. Association for Computational Linguistics.

Ondřej Pražák, Miloslav Konopík, and Jakub Sido. 2021. Multilingual Coreference Resolution with Harmonized Annotations. In *Proceedings of the International Conference on Recent Advances in Natural Language Processing (RANLP 2021)*, pages 1119–1123.

Ondřej Pražák and Miloslav Konopík. 2022. End-to-end Multilingual Coreference Resolution with Mention Head Prediction. In *Proceedings of the CRAC 2022 Shared Task on Multilingual Coreference Resolution*, pages 23–27. Association for Computational Linguistics.

Marta Recasens and Eduard H. Hovy. 2011. BLANC: Implementing the Rand index for coreference evaluation. *Natural Language Engineering*, 17(4):485–510.

Marta Recasens, Lluís Màrquez, Emili Sapena, M. Antònia Martí, Mariona Taulé, Véronique Hoste, Massimo Poesio, and Yannick Versley. 2010. SemEval-2010 task 1: Coreference resolution in multiple languages. In *Proceedings of the 5th International Workshop on Semantic Evaluation*, pages 1–8, Uppsala, Sweden. Association for Computational Linguistics.

Marta Recasens and M. Antònia Martí. 2010. AnCora-CO: Coreferentially Annotated Corpora for Spanish and Catalan. *Language Resources and Evaluation*, 44(4):315–345.

Milan Straka. 2018. UDPipe 2.0 prototype at CoNLL 2018 UD shared task. In *Proceedings of the CoNLL 2018 Shared Task: Multilingual Parsing from Raw Text to Universal Dependencies*, pages 197–207, Brussels, Belgium. Association for Computational Linguistics.

Milan Straka. 2023. ÚFAL CorPipe at CRAC 2023: Larger Context Improves Multilingual Coreference Resolution. In *Proceedings of the CRAC 2023 Shared Task on Multilingual Coreference Resolution*, pages 41–51.

Milan Straka and Jana Straková. 2022. ÚFAL CorPipe at CRAC 2022: Effectivity of Multilingual Models for Coreference Resolution. In *Proceedings of the CRAC 2022 Shared Task on Multilingual Coreference Resolution*, pages 28–37. Association for Computational Linguistics.

Mariona Taulé, M. Antònia Martí, and Marta Recasens. 2008. AnCora: Multilevel Annotated Corpora for Catalan and Spanish. In *Proceedings of the Sixth International Conference on Language Resources and Evaluation (LREC 2008)*, Marrakech, Morocco. European Language Resources Association.

Svetlana Toldova, Anna Roytberg, Alina Ladygina, Maria Vasilyeva, Ilya Azerkovich, Matvei Kurzukov, G. Sim, D.V. Gorshkov, A. Ivanova, Anna Nedoluzhko, and Yulia Grishina. 2014. Evaluating Anaphora and Coreference Resolution for Russian. In *Komp'juternaja lingvistika i intellektual'nye tehnologii. Po materialam ezhegodnoj Mezhdunarodnoj konferencii Dialog*, pages 681–695.

Shubham Toshniwal, Sam Wiseman, Allyson Ettinger, Karen Livescu, and Kevin Gimpel. 2020. Learning to Ignore: Long Document Coreference with Bounded Memory Neural Networks. In *Proceedings of the 2020 Conference on Empirical Methods in Natural Language Processing (EMNLP)*, pages 8519–8526, Online. Association for Computational Linguistics.

Shubham Toshniwal, Patrick Xia, Sam Wiseman, Karen Livescu, and Kevin Gimpel. 2021. On generalization in coreference resolution. In *Proceedings of the Fourth Workshop on Computational Models of Reference, Anaphora and Coreference*, pages 111–120, Punta Cana, Dominican Republic. Association for Computational Linguistics.

Don Tuggener. 2014. Coreference resolution evaluation for higher level applications. In *Proceedings of the 14th Conference of the European Chapter of the Association for Computational Linguistics, volume 2: Short Papers*, pages 231–235, Gothenburg, Sweden. Association for Computational Linguistics.

Olga Uryupina, Ron Artstein, Antonella Bristot, Federica Cavicchio, Francesca Delogu, Kepa J. Rodriguez, and Massimo Poesio. 2020. Annotating a broad range of anaphoric phenomena, in a variety of genres: the ARRAU Corpus. *Natural Language Engineering*, 26(1):95–128.

Noémi Vadász. 2022. Building a manually annotated Hungarian coreference corpus: Workflow and tools. In *Proceedings of the Fifth Workshop on Computational Models of Reference, Anaphora and Coreference*, pages 38–47, Gyeongju, Korea. Association for Computational Linguistics.

Marc Vilain, John Burger, John Aberdeen, Dennis Connolly, and Lynette Hirschman. 1995. A model-theoretic coreference scoring scheme. In *Sixth Message Understanding Conference (MUC-6): Proceedings of a Conference Held in Columbia, Maryland, November 6-8, 1995*.

Veronika Vincze, Klára Hegedűs, Alex Sliz-Nagy, and Richárd Farkas. 2018. SzegedKoref: A Hungarian coreference corpus. In *Proceedings of the Eleventh International Conference on Language Resources and Evaluation (LREC 2018)*, Miyazaki, Japan. European Language Resources Association.

Linting Xue, Noah Constant, Adam Roberts, Mihir Kale, Rami Al-Rfou, Aditya Siddhant, Aditya Barua, and Colin Raffel. 2021. mT5: A massively multilingual pre-trained text-to-text transformer. In *Proceedings of the 2021 Conference of the North American Chapter of the Association for Computational Linguistics: Human Language Technologies*, pages 483–498, Online. Association for Computational Linguistics.

Juntao Yu, Sopan Khosla, Nafise Sadat Moosavi, Silviu Paun, Sameer Pradhan, and Massimo Poesio. 2022. The Universal Anaphora Scorer. In *Proceedings of the Language Resources and Evaluation Conference*, pages 4873–4883, Marseille, France. European Language Resources Association.

Juntao Yu, Michal Novák, Abdulrahman Aloraini, Nafise Sadat Moosavi, Silviu Paun, Sameer Pradhan, and Massimo Poesio. 2023. The Universal Anaphora Scorer 2.0. In *Proceedings of the 15th International Conference on Computational Semantics (IWCS)*, Nancy, France. Association for Computational Linguistics.

Amir Zeldes. 2017. The GUM Corpus: Creating Multilayer Resources in the Classroom. *Language Resources and Evaluation*, 51(3):581–612.

Voldemaras Žitkus and Rita Butkienė. 2018. Coreference Annotation Scheme and Corpus for Lithuanian Language. In *Fifth International Conference on Social Networks Analysis, Management and Security, SNAMS 2018, Valencia, Spain, October 15-18, 2018*, pages 243–250. IEEE.

Zdeněk Žabokrtský, Miloslav Konopík, Anna Nedoluzhko, Michal Novák, Maciej Ogrodniczuk, Martin Popel, Ondřej Pražák, Jakub Sido, Daniel Zeman, and Yilun Zhu. 2022. Findings of the Shared Task on Multilingual Coreference Resolution. In *Proceedings of the CRAC 2022 Shared Task on Multilingual Coreference Resolution*, pages 1–17, Gyeongju, Korea. Association for Computational Linguistics.

A Data References

Catalan	AnCora	ca_ancora	(Taulé et al., 2008; Recasens and Martí, 2010)
Czech	PCEDT	cs_pcedt	(Nedoluzhko et al., 2016)
Czech	PDT	cs_pdt	(Hajič et al., 2020)
English	GUM	en_gum	(Zeldes, 2017)
English	ParCorFull	en_parcorfull	(Lapshinova-Koltunski et al., 2018)
French	Democrat	fr_democrat	(Landragin, 2021)
German	ParCorFull	de_parcorfull	(Lapshinova-Koltunski et al., 2018)
German	PotsdamCC	de_potsdam	(Bourgonje and Stede, 2020)
Hungarian	KorKor	hu_korkor	(Vadász, 2022)
Hungarian	SzegedKoref	hu_szeged	(Vincze et al., 2018)
Lithuanian	LCC	lt_lcc	(Žitkus and Butkienė, 2018)
Norwegian	Bokmål NARC	no_bokmaalnarc	(Mæhlum et al., 2022)
Norwegian	Nynorsk NARC	no_nynorsknarc	(Mæhlum et al., 2022)
Polish	PCC	pl_pcc	(Ogrodniczuk et al., 2013, 2015)
Russian	RuCor	ru_rucor	(Toldova et al., 2014)
Spanish	AnCora	es_ancora	(Taulé et al., 2008; Recasens and Martí, 2010)
Turkish	ITCC	tr_itcc	(Pamay and Eryiğit, 2018)

B Partial CoNLL results by head UPOS

system	NOUN	PRON	PROPN	DET	ADJ	VERB	ADV	NUM
CorPipe	**72.21**	**77.05**	**76.33**	**51.58**	**44.38**	**40.13**	33.88	37.44
Anonymous	68.25	72.70	70.84	50.98	38.42	34.15	**35.91**	**41.86**
Ondfa	66.98	71.27	70.16	48.52	33.78	24.98	33.76	40.82
McGill	62.67	68.07	63.76	51.03	39.00	23.68	32.87	28.60
DeepBlueAI	59.54	65.05	60.08	40.34	36.57	17.57	28.26	31.68
DFKI-Adapt	57.80	64.02	61.82	39.53	26.72	14.71	21.29	33.03
Morfbase	55.39	61.74	58.45	44.61	28.58	20.74	30.26	29.17
BASELINE	51.82	57.79	56.32	33.89	25.80	14.12	19.43	27.51
DFKI-MPrompt	50.07	57.37	54.84	42.28	21.37	12.30	25.36	17.81

Table 7: CoNLL F1 score evaluated only on entities with heads of a given UPOS. In both the gold and prediction files we deleted some entities before running the evaluation. We kept only entities with at least one mention with a given head UPOS (universal part of speech tag). For the purpose of this analysis, if the head node had deprel=flat children, their UPOS tags were considered as well, so for example in "Mr./NOUN Brown/PROPN" both NOUN and PROPN were taken as head UPOS, so the entity with this mention will be reported in both columns NOUN and PROPN. Otherwise, the CoNLL F1 scores are the same as in the primary metric, i.e. an unweighted average over all datasets, partial-match, without singletons. Note that when distinguishing entities into events and nominal entities, the VERB column can be considered as an approximation of the performance on events. One of the limitations of this approach is that copula is not treated as head in the Universal Dependencies, so e.g. phrase *She is nice* is not considered for the VERB column, but for the ADJ column (head of the phrase is *nice*).

system	NOUN	PRON	PROPN	DET	ADJ	VERB	ADV	NUM
CorPipe	**63.51**	**65.25**	**63.85**	**52.93**	**49.85**	**50.48**	**51.24**	**50.30**
Anonymous	57.32	59.16	57.80	49.09	46.65	46.39	46.02	46.08
Ondfa	56.39	58.32	57.08	45.55	42.93	42.79	42.64	42.48
McGill	53.13	55.73	52.97	42.50	39.46	39.50	38.79	38.94
DeepBlueAI	50.43	51.93	49.63	40.39	37.60	38.02	37.36	37.14
DFKI-Adapt	48.56	50.95	50.60	34.66	32.05	32.32	31.76	31.59
Morfbase	47.08	48.93	49.23	36.41	33.90	33.92	33.36	33.19
BASELINE	40.50	43.28	45.60	30.62	27.74	28.48	27.74	27.65
DFKI-MPrompt	39.56	43.31	42.67	29.20	26.53	26.64	26.22	26.33

Table 8: CoNLL F1 score evaluated only on mentions with heads of a given UPOS. In both the gold and prediction files we deleted some mentions before running the evaluation. We kept only mentions with a given head UPOS (again considering also deprel=flat children).

C Statistics of the submitted systems on concatenation of all test sets

	entities				distribution of lengths				
system	total	per 1k	length		1	2	3	4	5+
	count	words	max	avg.	[%]	[%]	[%]	[%]	[%]
gold	44,806	107	509	2.0	61.7	22.0	6.7	3.2	6.5
Anonymous	46,367	110	232	2.0	64.0	20.3	6.7	3.0	6.0
BASELINE	14,059	33	237	3.8	0.0	57.7	17.3	7.6	17.4
CorPipe	47,054	112	540	2.0	62.6	21.0	6.8	3.2	6.3
DFKI-Adapt	14,808	35	230	3.8	0.0	56.6	17.7	8.0	17.7
DFKI-MPrompt	12,884	31	85	3.7	0.0	55.5	18.2	8.6	17.7
DeepBlueAI	14,635	35	165	3.9	0.0	54.1	18.4	8.4	19.1
McGill	44,059	105	425	1.9	67.8	17.7	5.8	2.7	6.0
Morfbase	15,118	36	92	3.6	0.0	56.9	18.2	8.2	16.8
Ondfa	55,232	131	135	1.8	70.8	16.3	5.2	2.4	5.3

Table 9: Statistics on coreference entities. The total number of entities and the average number of entities per 1000 tokens in the running text. The maximum and average entity "length", i.e., the number of mentions in the entity. Distribution of entity lengths (singletons have length = 1). The systems are sorted alphabetically. We can see that the Ondfa system notably overgenerates, i.e. predicts more entities than in the gold data. On the contrary, DeepBlueAI, DFKI-Adapt, BASELINE, DFKI-MPrompt, and Morfbase undergenerate and predict on average longer entities (i.e. with more mentions) than in the gold data. The best two systems, CorPipe and Anonymous, have the statistics similar to the gold data.

system	mentions				distribution of lengths					
	total	per 1k	length		0	1	2	3	4	5+
	count	words	max	avg.	[%]	[%]	[%]	[%]	[%]	[%]
gold	66,520	158	100	3.1	8.3	45.1	18.7	8.0	3.9	15.9
Anonymous	87,664	209	101	3.3	6.7	41.5	20.5	9.3	4.7	17.3
BASELINE	53,063	126	29	2.2	9.9	50.0	19.0	7.2	3.3	10.6
CorPipe	91,081	217	163	3.2	6.5	41.4	20.8	9.5	4.8	16.9
DFKI-Adapt	56,749	135	29	2.3	9.4	49.0	19.2	7.4	3.5	11.5
DFKI-MPrompt	47,796	114	71	2.9	10.7	50.2	17.2	5.8	2.7	13.2
DeepBlueAI	57,329	136	26	2.3	9.2	48.3	19.5	7.7	3.7	11.7
McGill	81,989	195	20	2.3	7.1	43.8	21.8	9.8	5.0	12.5
Morfbase	54,668	130	29	2.3	9.6	48.8	19.0	7.4	3.5	11.6
Ondfa	97,081	231	29	2.6	6.0	49.7	17.6	7.8	4.3	14.5

Table 10: Statistics on non-singleton mentions. The total number of mentions and the average number of mentions per 1000 words of running text. The maximum and average mention length, i.e., the number of nonempty nodes (words) in the mention. Distribution of mention lengths (zeros have length = 0). We can see that Ondfa, CorPipe, and Anonymous notably overgenerate mentions, i.e. predict more mentions than in the gold data, but these are the three best systems, so it seems a reasonable strategy. Note that CorPipe is the only system that has higher Recall than Precision in MUC and CEAF-e, according to Table 4. The average length of mentions predicted by Ondfa is lower than in the gold data (and it is caused by the single-word mentions in some datasets). CorPipe and Anonymous are the only two systems that predict long mentions (5+ words) more frequently than in the gold data.

system	mentions				distribution of lengths					
	total	per 1k	length		0	1	2	3	4	5+
	count	words	max	avg.	[%]	[%]	[%]	[%]	[%]	[%]
gold	24,961	59	81	3.5	1.3	30.7	25.1	13.6	7.4	21.9
Anonymous	3,088	7	57	3.9	0.0	31.2	25.3	12.3	7.8	23.4
BASELINE	0	0	0	0.0	0.0	0.0	0.0	0.0	0.0	0.0
CorPipe	2,674	6	78	3.7	0.1	31.5	25.7	12.2	8.2	22.4
DFKI-Adapt	0	0	0	0.0	0.0	0.0	0.0	0.0	0.0	0.0
DFKI-MPrompt	0	0	0	0.0	0.0	0.0	0.0	0.0	0.0	0.0
DeepBlueAI	0	0	0	0.0	0.0	0.0	0.0	0.0	0.0	0.0
McGill	3,160	8	15	2.9	0.0	33.7	27.3	12.7	7.6	18.7
Morfbase	0	0	0	0.0	0.0	0.0	0.0	0.0	0.0	0.0
Ondfa	3,226	8	21	3.3	0.1	32.5	26.1	12.2	7.2	21.9

Table 11: Statistics on singleton mentions. See the caption of Table 10 for details. Only four systems (Anonymous, CorPipe, McGill, and Ondfa) attempt to predict singletons and none of them as frequently as in the gold data. Note that singletons are not annotated in all the (gold) datasets.

	mention type [%]			distribution of head UPOS [%]								
system	w/empty	w/gap	non-tree	NOUN	PRON	PROPN	DET	ADJ	VERB	ADV	NUM	other
gold	10.5	0.6	2.0	44.1	23.3	14.7	7.1	2.7	4.2	1.2	0.5	2.2
Anonymous	8.5	0.0	3.4	51.9	19.1	13.6	5.8	2.5	3.6	1.0	0.6	1.8
BASELINE	11.2	0.0	1.8	39.0	26.6	16.1	8.4	2.5	3.8	1.2	0.3	2.1
CorPipe	8.1	0.0	2.6	52.9	18.6	13.8	5.7	2.6	3.2	0.9	0.6	1.7
DFKI-Adapt	10.8	0.0	1.8	40.3	25.8	15.9	8.0	2.5	3.9	1.2	0.4	2.0
DFKI-MPrompt	12.6	0.0	2.0	37.7	29.0	14.7	9.1	1.7	4.0	1.1	0.2	2.5
DeepBlueAI	10.6	0.0	1.9	41.4	25.2	15.3	7.9	2.7	3.8	1.3	0.4	2.0
McGill	8.0	0.0	2.1	51.5	20.4	13.6	6.3	2.4	2.6	1.0	0.6	1.6
Morfbase	11.0	0.0	1.8	40.1	26.1	16.1	8.1	2.4	3.8	1.1	0.4	1.9
Ondfa	7.3	0.1	2.0	54.1	17.6	14.2	5.4	2.5	2.8	1.0	0.9	1.5

Table 12: Detailed statistics on non-singleton mentions. The left part of the table shows the percentage of: mentions with at least one empty node (w/empty); mentions with at least one gap, i.e. discontinuous mentions (w/gap); and non-treelet mentions, i.e. mentions not forming a connected subgraph in the dependency tree (non-tree). Note that these three types of mentions may be overlapping. We can see that none of the systems attempts to predict discontinuous mentions (the 0.1% of such mentions in Ondfa seems to be rather a technical error). The right part of the table shows the distribution of mentions based on the universal part-of-speech tag (UPOS) of the head word. Note that this distribution has to be interpreted with the total number of non-singleton mentions predicted (as reported in Table 10) in mind. For example, only 18.6% of mentions predicted by CorPipe are pronominal (head=PRON), while there are 23.3% of pronominal mentions in the gold data. However, UDPipe predicts actually more pronominal mentions (16941) than in the gold data (15500).

D Statistics of the submitted systems on cs_pcedt

	entities				distribution of lengths				
system	total	per 1k	length		1	2	3	4	5+
	count	words	max	avg.	[%]	[%]	[%]	[%]	[%]
gold	2,533	45	84	3.2	7.2	60.1	13.8	6.2	12.8
Anonymous	2,804	50	74	2.9	21.0	47.5	14.2	5.4	11.8
BASELINE	1,963	35	77	3.5	0.0	61.7	16.4	6.9	15.0
CorPipe	2,918	52	81	3.0	20.5	47.5	13.4	5.8	12.7
DFKI-Adapt	2,034	36	73	3.6	0.0	60.4	16.2	7.5	15.9
DFKI-MPrompt	1,767	32	36	3.4	0.0	58.7	18.8	8.1	14.3
DeepBlueAI	2,069	37	71	3.6	0.0	60.7	15.9	7.2	16.3
McGill	2,627	47	83	2.8	33.4	39.4	11.2	4.5	11.5
Morfbase	2,038	36	37	3.4	0.0	60.7	17.0	8.0	14.3
Ondfa	2,844	51	74	3.0	23.9	45.4	13.0	5.3	12.3

Table 13: Statistics on coreference entities in cs_pcedt.

system	mentions				distribution of lengths					
	total	per 1k	length		0	1	2	3	4	5+
	count	words	max	avg.	[%]	[%]	[%]	[%]	[%]	[%]
gold	7,905	141	61	3.7	19.8	27.9	18.0	8.8	3.9	21.5
Anonymous	7,594	135	60	3.7	20.5	28.7	17.8	8.1	3.8	21.1
BASELINE	6,931	124	23	2.6	21.1	29.6	19.5	9.1	4.0	16.7
CorPipe	8,083	144	59	3.7	19.0	28.5	18.3	9.0	4.3	21.0
DFKI-Adapt	7,292	130	23	2.7	20.3	29.2	19.7	9.4	4.2	17.2
DFKI-MPrompt	6,050	108	61	3.5	23.7	31.1	16.7	6.0	2.9	19.4
DeepBlueAI	7,420	132	21	2.8	20.3	28.5	19.4	9.3	4.5	18.0
McGill	6,448	115	16	2.2	22.8	29.2	19.8	10.0	4.8	13.5
Morfbase	6,843	122	26	2.7	21.4	29.5	18.9	9.2	4.2	16.8
Ondfa	7,745	138	22	3.0	19.6	28.7	19.1	9.4	4.5	18.7

Table 14: Statistics on non-singleton mentions in cs_pcedt.

system	mentions				distribution of lengths					
	total	per 1k	length		0	1	2	3	4	5+
	count	words	max	avg.	[%]	[%]	[%]	[%]	[%]	[%]
gold	182	3	34	3.3	20.9	21.4	18.1	11.0	8.2	20.3
Anonymous	590	11	47	4.5	9.0	18.3	24.9	15.6	7.3	24.9
BASELINE	0	0	0	0.0	0.0	0.0	0.0	0.0	0.0	0.0
CorPipe	598	11	30	4.0	12.4	13.4	26.1	14.0	9.2	24.9
DFKI-Adapt	0	0	0	0.0	0.0	0.0	0.0	0.0	0.0	0.0
DFKI-MPrompt	0	0	0	0.0	0.0	0.0	0.0	0.0	0.0	0.0
DeepBlueAI	0	0	0	0.0	0.0	0.0	0.0	0.0	0.0	0.0
McGill	877	16	15	2.0	15.5	40.7	19.4	8.4	5.4	10.6
Morfbase	0	0	0	0.0	0.0	0.0	0.0	0.0	0.0	0.0
Ondfa	679	12	22	3.7	12.8	21.8	19.0	12.7	7.7	26.1

Table 15: Statistics on singleton mentions in cs_pcedt.

system	mention type [%]			distribution of head UPOS [%]								
	w/empty	w/gap	non-tree	NOUN	PRON	PROPN	DET	ADJ	VERB	ADV	NUM	other
gold	25.9	0.7	4.5	46.2	25.5	6.7	13.2	0.9	2.7	1.6	0.7	2.5
Anonymous	26.3	0.0	2.4	46.6	24.2	7.0	15.9	1.2	2.4	1.5	0.5	0.7
BASELINE	24.7	0.0	1.9	47.1	24.8	7.6	15.4	1.1	1.5	1.6	0.6	0.2
CorPipe	24.6	0.0	1.7	48.9	22.5	7.2	15.3	1.3	2.1	1.6	0.6	0.5
DFKI-Adapt	24.0	0.0	1.8	48.1	24.2	7.4	15.0	1.1	1.8	1.7	0.7	0.2
DFKI-MPrompt	29.0	0.0	2.1	42.8	28.3	6.7	17.7	1.1	1.4	1.3	0.3	0.3
DeepBlueAI	24.2	0.0	1.6	48.2	23.9	7.3	15.2	1.1	2.1	1.6	0.5	0.2
McGill	25.9	0.0	1.3	48.1	26.7	6.7	15.0	0.9	0.8	1.2	0.6	0.1
Morfbase	25.1	0.0	1.8	46.9	25.3	7.2	15.4	1.3	1.7	1.6	0.5	0.1
Ondfa	23.9	0.0	1.7	49.2	23.2	7.4	15.0	1.2	1.4	1.7	0.6	0.3

Table 16: Detailed statistics on non-singleton mentions in cs_pcedt.

Multilingual coreference resolution: Adapt and Generate

Tatiana Anikina*, **Natalia Skachkova***, **Anna Mokhova**
DFKI / Saarland Informatics Campus, Saarbrücken, Germany
tatiana.anikina@dfki.de; natalia.skachkova@dfki.de
annmo00006@stud.uni-saarland.de

Abstract

The paper presents two multilingual coreference resolution systems submitted for the CRAC Shared Task 2023. The *DFKI-Adapt* system achieves 61.86 F1 score on the shared task test data, outperforming the official baseline by 4.9 F1 points. This system uses a combination of different features and training settings, including character embeddings, adapter modules, joint pre-training and loss-based re-training. We provide evaluation for each of the settings on 12 different datasets and compare the results. The other submission *DFKI-MPrompt* uses a novel approach that involves prompting for mention generation. Although the scores achieved by this model are lower compared to the baseline, the method shows a new way of approaching the coreference task and provides good results with just five epochs of training.

1 Introduction

Coreference resolution is a task of finding all mentions referring to the same physical or abstract entity in the given piece of text. E.g., in sentences *"I've never been to London before. But I heard it is a lovely place"* the words *London* and *it* both refer to the real-world entity *the city of London*, and are called an antecedent and an anaphor respectively. Coreference resolution includes two sub-tasks that can be done either in a pipeline manner, or jointly: mention detection and mention clustering. They are quite challenging: (i) antecedents can be split; (ii) mentions can be discontinuous; (iii) one needs to consider the semantics of the context; (iv) there are long-distance coreference relations, etc. Coreference resolution contributes to the correct automatic text understanding, and is important for many NLP tasks, including text summarization and paraphrasing, information extraction, machine translation, question answering, etc.

*Equal contribution

The CRAC-2023 shared task (Žabokrtský et al., 2023) focuses on multilingual coreference resolution. However, the majority of language models are still being created for English, e.g., about 70% of the oral papers at ACL 2021 presented models evaluated only on English (Ruder et al., 2022). The problem is that many languages, even some of the big ones, do not have enough labeled training data, especially for specific tasks. Another issue is that training a separate model for each separate language when the task stays the same can be too time- and resource-consuming, especially when the model is large. A typical solution to this is transfer learning, when a model trained on some language(s) or task(s) is adapted to work for another one. In this paper we present our approach to transfer learning for multilingual coreference resolution.

Our first submission *DFKI-Adapt* presents a novel approach which combines joint pre-training, combined datasets for related languages, loss-based re-training, character embeddings and adapters. Our second submission *DFKI-MPrompt* integrates prompting. Prompting is a way of eliciting the desired output from a large language model (LLM). It was first introduced by Brown et al. (2020). The main motivation behind prompting is to avoid computationally expensive fine-tuning of LLMs, as they contain billions of parameters. Moreover, such models already incorporate lots of various knowledge, therefore we can simply add demonstrations to our input to help the model "understand" what we want and produce the desired output.

To summarize, our contributions are as follows.

- We investigate how to combine the existing data, features and fine-tuning approaches to improve the baseline results without larger models or additional data.
- We check if knowledge accumulated in large multilingual language models can be extracted

Proceedings of the CRAC 2023 Shared Task on Multilingual Coreference Resolution, pages 19–33
December 7, 2023

using prompt fine-tuning to perform mention detection, and if this method can compete with the state-of-the-art one.

- Some of the approaches we try have never been used for the given task before, and can be of interest for the community.

2 Related work

In this section we outline the main achievements in the area of multilingual coreference resolution, and present the approaches that are similar to our work.

Most progress in the area of multilingual coreference resolution was made due to the introduction of shared tasks. SemEval-2010 Task 1 (Recasens et al., 2010) was designed to evaluate and compare methods of coreference resolution in six languages (Catalan, Dutch, English, German, Italian, and Spanish) and used four different metrics: MUC (Vilain et al., 1995), B^3 (Bagga and Baldwin, 1998), CEAF (Luo, 2005) and BLANC (Recasens and Hovy, 2011). There were six systems submitted for this task, all of them rely on feature extraction and machine learning algorithms, like maximum entropy, decision trees, support vector machines (SVM), etc. Only two systems, UBIU (Zhekova and Kübler, 2010) and SUCRE (Kobdani and Schütze, 2010) work for all the languages.

CoNLL-2012 (Pradhan et al., 2012) was dedicated to predicting coreference in the OntoNotes corpus (Pradhan et al., 2007) which includes data in English, Chinese, and Arabic. The evaluation metrics included metrics used for SemEval-2010 and a CoNLL score representing an unweighted average of MUC, B^3 and entity based CEAF. There were 16 systems submitted for CoNLL-2012. The majority of them combine machine learning approaches mentioned earlier with the rule-based ones. The latter are typically used for mention detection. The best performing systems also heavily rely on feature engineering. As far as we can judge, most of the systems assume training a separate model for each language.

In contrast to the previous shared tasks, CRAC-2022 (Žabokrtský et al., 2022) offered much more data in different languages. The CorefUD 1.0 collection (Nedoluzhko et al., 2022) included 13 datasets in Czech, English, Polish, French, Russian, German, Catalan, Spanish, Lithuanian and Hungarian which were harmonized to the same annotation scheme and data format. The primary evaluation metric was the CoNLL score. The organizers offered a strong Transformer-based baseline (Pražák et al., 2021), which was also used for the current shared task. There were eight systems submitted.The absolute majority use deep learning approaches and rely on large pre-trained models. Importantly, most of the systems present cross-lingual models trained on all the multilingual data.

It is actually difficult to compare all these models in terms of numbers and judge how much progress has been made since SemEval-2010 for multilingual coreference resolution. First, the models were trained on quite different data. Second, despite the unification of the annotations, the definition of a mention varies across the datasets. Third, the evaluation criteria are also different, in the first place for mention boundaries detection.

Our *DFKI-Adapt* system uses a combination of different settings that includes pre-trained adapters. As far as we know, adapters (Houlsby et al., 2019; Rebuffi et al., 2017) have not been well researched for multilingual coreference resolution. Adapters represent a small amount of additional parameters that can be added as trainable task-specific weights at each layer of the transformer architecture (Vaswani et al., 2017). They have been successful on a variety tasks including speech recognition (Hou et al., 2021), cross-lingual transfer (Parovic et al., 2022) and classification tasks (Lee et al., 2022; Anikina, 2023; Metheniti et al., 2023) but there is very little research on using adapters for coreference resolution and the only work that we are aware of uses parallel data for training (Tang and Hardmeier, 2023).

The idea of prompting LLMs for the task of coreference resolution is relatively new. There are not so many papers on this topic. E.g., Perez et al. (2021) do few-shot prompting to resolve anaphora that requires commonsense knowledge using the Winograd Schema Challenge (WSC) corpus (Levesque et al., 2012). Min et al. (2022) perform similar experiments on the WSC and Wino-Grande (Sakaguchi et al., 2021) data, and Yang et al. (2022) - on ECB+ (Cybulska and Vossen, 2014). Le et al. (2022) and Agrawal et al. (2022) try prompting for coreference resolution in scientific protocols and medical domain, respectively. Lin et al. (2022) experiment with few- and zero-shot anaphora resolution in the multilingual XWinograd corpus (Tikhonov and Ryabinin, 2021). In contrast to our approach, all these models do not perform prompt fine-tuning, instead they typically include a few demonstrations into their prompts (therefore few-shot) and use much larger models, like XGLM (Lin et al., 2022), GPT-2 (Radford et al., 2019), GPT-3 (Brown et al., 2020) or InstructGPT (Ouyang et al., 2022). Moreover, we use prompting only for mention generation. A somewhat similar approach but without prompting was presented by Kalyanpur et al. (2020), who used the *T5* model (Raffel et al., 2020) to generate semantic roles when doing frame-semantic parsing.

3 Data

All our experiments are done using an officially provided public version of the CorefUD 1.1 data, which extends CorefUD 1.0 with new datasets in Hungarian, Norwegian and Turkish. In total, this version of CorefUD consists of 17 datasets in 12 languages. The datasets vary a lot in their sizes (see Table 7 in the Appendix B). Moreover, they represent different language families and subgroups with very different grammars and vocabularies. Also, the datasets differ in how markables are defined, e.g., some datasets omit singletons, others may annotate verbal phrases, if they are antecedents of anaphoric noun phrases (Žabokrtský et al., 2022). All this makes it very challenging to build a single model working well for all the given languages.

Intuitively, the quality of mention extraction and subsequent coreference resolution depends not only on the training data size, but also on length and complexity of the sentences and mentions, the number of mentions (including nested) in a sentence, the amount of unique named entities, etc. To get an idea about difficulty of the task, we collected some basic statistical facts about the relevant data properties. This information can be found in Table 8 in the Appendix B.

4 Multilingual coreference resolution with DFKI-Adapt

Our submission *DFKI-Adapt* is based on the baseline provided by the organizers but extended in different ways to accommodate the multi-lingual nature of the task. The *DFKI-Adapt* system integrates character embeddings, joint pre-training and fine-tuning on the datasets of the related languages. It also includes additional re-training on the documents with the higher loss and uses adapter modules that were pre-trained for each dataset.

The goal of the *DFKI-Adapt* submission is to demonstrate how one could get a substantial improvement over the baseline (+4.9 F1 points on the test and +9.07 F1 on the development partitions) without any additional data or larger models, just by leveraging the existing annotations. All experiments are performed with standard multilingual BERT and the official CRAC data. The following sections introduce our baselines, the experiments with individual settings and the final results achieved by *DFKI-Adapt*. Since the test data are not publicly available our evaluation is performed on the CRAC development set. The evaluation results on 12 datasets for different languages[1] are summarized in Table 1. The more detailed analysis with different coreference evaluation metrics is reported in Tables 3-6 in the Appendix A.

4.1 Baselines

We consider three different baselines for our system. Firstly, we use the official baseline of the shared task which was published by the organizers (*CRAC-baseline*). Secondly, we train a single joint coreference model based on multilingual BERT and use it to predict coreference chains for each dataset (*mbert-joined*). Thirdly, we train a separate model for each language and dataset present in the shared task (*mbert-separate*). The results in Table 1 demonstrate that *mbert-joined* consistently outperforms *mbert-separate* indicating that joint training on the combination of all datasets is a good strategy for coreference resolution. The main baseline to which we compare different settings in the following sections is the official *CRAC-baseline*.

4.2 Adapters

We add adapters to multilingual BERT and then fine-tune them for each dataset separately. Then we load the pre-trained adapters and train a new coreference resolution model for each dataset from scratch but with the pre-trained adapter weights. In one setting, *task-adapters-frozen*, we do not further train the adapters, while the rest of the model is being tuned on the coreference resolution task. In another setting, *task-adapters-tuned*, we continue training the adapters together with the rest of the model. According to the experimental results

[1]For some languages several datasets were available and we selected a single dataset for each language as a representative. Although the differences between the datasets can also occur within a single language, we evaluated one dataset per language given the limited time, resources and the goal of comparing different languages rather than the datasets. Further details can be found in the Appendix A.

Dataset	mbert-joined	mbert-separate	char-embed	joined-pre-training	combined-datasets	loss-re-training	task-adapters-frozen	task-adapters-tuned	DFKI-Adapt	CRAC-baseline
ca_ancora	**68.97**	65.06	66.56	68.72	66.29	65.59	66.19	61.99	68.34	65.60
cs_pdt	66.35	65.30	67.45	68.32	66.62	65.36	66.35	61.18	**68.60**	65.66
en_gum	65.80	52.01	54.05	62.41	35.25	51.38	51.49	47.54	**69.63**	66.87
fr_democrat	59.74	58.85	58.88	60.97	61.09	57.81	57.88	52.50	**62.34**	57.22
de_potsdamcc	65.77	58.92	55.16	62.03	67.12	59.77	64.28	60.27	**69.29**	56.07
hu_szegedkoref	59.78	59.98	59.53	62.29	60.42	60.13	57.39	53.70	**62.60**	58.96
lt_lcc	71.22	69.09	69.55	73.18	**75.76**	69.47	68.05	64.95	73.08	66.96
no_bokmaal	69.81	68.47	69.11	72.26	69.09	67.65	68.83	64.53	**72.45**	58.44
pl_pcc	65.41	63.64	65.32	**66.38**	66.21	63.74	64.30	59.44	65.89	64.17
ru_rucor	62.08	62.11	63.84	66.54	64.58	63.26	61.73	57.97	**67.50**	63.04
es_ancora	67.00	66.37	67.99	69.82	66.64	66.29	66.99	62.53	**70.07**	67.00
tr_itcc	31.66	31.35	17.98	30.80	33.88	23.28	20.68	6.91	**37.80**	16.15

Table 1: CoNLL F1 scores on the development data. The best performing setting is in bold

shown in Table 1, for *task-adapters-frozen* the results differ significantly between the datasets. E.g., we can see that the model trained on the German data gives an improvement of +8.21 F1 points compared to the *CRAC-baseline* and for Turkish the improvement is +4.53 F1 points. Polish and Czech also have small gains in performance when using pre-trained adapters (+0.13 and +0.69 F1 points correspondingly). However, Hungarian has a drop of -1.57 F1 points compared to the CRAC baseline.

We also observe that using pre-trained adapters and then freezing them consistently outperforms the version with tunable adapters. Compared to the CRAC baseline the latter model underperforms by 4.39 F1 points on average. We notice that using language-specific pre-trained adapters gives model a "warm start" and it starts with a slightly better performance, e.g., the ratio of the correctly predicted to gold mention spans is higher than if we start training the model from scratch, without any pre-trained adapters.

4.3 Character embeddings

For character embeddings we consider 273 characters which include the alphabet letters of all relevant languages plus some additional symbols such as currency or copyright signs. A symbol has to occur more than 5 times in the training set in order to be included in our list of the frequent characters. After making the character list we run bi-LSTM to encode every token in the data.

Then in the coreference resolution model we add an extra layer that projects character embeddings from 300 to 100 dimensions and concatenate the character embeddings of the start and the end of each span with the corresponding BERT embeddings. We observe that adding character embeddings gives a small boost in performance compared to the CRAC baseline (+0.77 F1 points on average). Interestingly, the only two languages which show a decrease in performance are German and English, all other languages show some improvement and the largest gains are attributed to Norwegian +10.67 F1 and Lithuanian +2.59 F1.

4.4 Joined pre-training

As discussed in Section 3, the available datasets are quite different. However, since in all the cases the task is to identify and cluster coreferent mentions we believe that patterns relevant for coreference resolution in one language may prove to be helpful for another. Hence, we pre-train one multilingual BERT model on all datasets combined together and then we continue fine-tuning this model on each language separately. We restrict the number of the pre-training steps to 100,000 and leave all other hyper-parameters unchanged. This setting with the joined pre-training is beneficial for all languages and it brings an average improvement of +4.8 F1 points on the development data compared to the CRAC baseline.

4.5 Combined datasets

In the *combined-datasets* setting we test whether combining the training sets of the related languages can boost the performance. E.g., for Spanish we combine it with the training sets for other Romance languages that include Catalan and French, and for Czech we combine both datasets for this language (*cs_pdt* and *cs_pcedt*) together with the annotations for Polish and Russian. Note that we do not adjust for any differences in the dataset size and do not balance the amount of samples that might have negatively impacted the performance in some of the cases (e.g., Spanish and Catalan data have more than 1,000 documents each, whereas French has only 50 documents).

The results in Table 1 show that combining the datasets of the related languages is a good approach in many cases, although it seems to help some languages more than the others (e.g., it brings +11.05 F1 points for *de_potsdamcc* but only +0.96 F1 for *cs_pdt*). We notice that this method is especially beneficial for those cases where we have a relatively small number of annotated documents (e.g., French with only 50 documents in the training set and Lithuanian with 80). Also, perhaps due to the differences in the annotation format, for some languages we notice a significant drop in performance when we train on the combined datasets. E.g., the model trained on the *en_gum* data combined with *en_parcorfull*, *de_potsdamcc* and *de_parcorfull* datasets shows poor performance in our experiments, achieving only 35.25 F1. Further ablation studies and error analysis are needed to find the exact cause of this issue.

In some cases finding datasets in related languages is not possible and we combine the corpora based on other linguistic similarities, e.g., both Hungarian and Turkish are agglutinative languages and both of them benefit from the combined datasets (see Table 1).

4.6 Loss-based re-training

In the *loss-re-training* setting we store the loss associated with each document per epoch and at the end of each epoch we sort the documents by their corresponding losses and take the 10% of the most difficult documents (i.e., the ones with the highest loss) to continue additional training. This means that we effectively fine-tune our models on particularly difficult instances.

This approach brings an average improvement of +0.63% F1 points across all datasets, as shown in Table 1, but the gains differ between the languages. E.g., the *lt_lcc* and *tr_itcc* data show substantial improvements with the loss-based re-training: +2.51 and +7.13 F1 points respectively. However, some datasets (e.g., *es_ancora*, *cs_pdt* and *en_gum*) show worse performance.

The discrepancy is potentially caused by the imbalance in the amount of the available training data between the datasets. The datasets with the fewer documents (e.g., *tr_itcc* with 19 and *lt_lcc* with 80) seem to benefit from the loss-based re-training while other datasets with relatively large amount of documents do not benefit from it (e.g., *es_ancora* with 1,080 documents or *cs_pdt* with 2,533). In the future we would like to explore this fine-tuning approach in more detail and apply it to different low-resource settings using various metrics to order and select difficult documents (e.g., ordering them by entropy or surprisal).

4.7 DFKI-Adapt

Our submission *DFKI-Adapt* combines the best-performing configurations as described above. It includes *joined-pre-training* for 100,000 steps together with the *combined-datasets* setting for fine-tuning on the combined training data for the related languages. It also integrates character embeddings as in the *char-embedding* configuration. Additionally, we fine-tune each model on the 10% of the most difficult documents per dataset (as in *loss-re-training*) and we also include the pre-trained adapter modules as in *task-adapters-frozen*.

DFKI-Adapt consistently outperforms all three baselines (*mbert-joined*, *mbert-separate* and *CRAC-baseline*) and for most of the languages it gives the best performance on the development set, although for some datasets (e.g., *pl_pcc* and *lt_lcc*) other configurations such as *joined-pre-training* or *combined-datasets* perform slightly better than *DFKI-Adapt* (see Table 1 for comparison). On the official test set our *DFKI-Adapt* system achieves 61.86 CoNLL F1 score (+4.89 F1 points compared to the CRAC baseline) and on the development set it achieves 68.06 CoNLL F1 score (+9.07 F1 points compared to the baseline).

All our models are trained on either NVIDIA RTX A6000 with 48 GB memory or NVIDIA A100-SXM4 with 40 GB memory. We use the hyper-parameter settings as defined in the baseline configuration file[2] and train the models for the same amount of epochs. For the models that use adapters we set the BERT learning rate to 1e-05 and the task learning rate to 2e-4. We set the dropout rate to 0.4 and the mention loss coefficient to 0. For optimizing the network we employ *AdamW* and a linear schedule with warm-up.

[2]See `https://github.com/ondfa/coref-multiling/` for the configuration details and the hyper-parameter settings.

5 Multilingual coreference resolution with DFKI-MPrompt

In this section we first present our approach to mention identification as generation, then explain how we adapt the baseline to work with the mentions generated by our model. We discuss the results obtained by our system, analyse the mistakes and outline possible improvements.

5.1 Mention generation

The absolute majority of modern coreference resolution models, including the baseline provided for this shared task, use span ranking with pruning to identify mentions. As pointed out in Section 3, the results depend on many factors, such as how the markables are defined in the dataset, the dataset size, domain and language, etc. E.g., the baseline[3] reaches up to 85.16 F1 in mention identification on the *no_nynorsk* and only about 54.65 F1 on the *tr_itcc* development data. Correct mention identification is crucial for successful coreference resolution. The same baseline achieves the F1 score of only 38.17 in coreference resolution on the *de_parcorfull* development data, if it has to predict the mentions. However, if the gold mentions are given, the F1 score reaches 91.90 points on the same data.

Motivated by the recent success of prompting LLMs for various downstream NLP tasks, we decide to try casting mention identification problem as a generation task using a simple prefix prompt. Theoretically, mention generation offers certain advantages in comparison with the span-ranking approach, e.g., (a) no pruning is required; (b) it is possible to generate discontinuous and nested mentions; (c) both input and output are in natural language and therefore are easy to analyze for a human. Moreover, as far as we are aware, no one has tried mention generation as a way to identify mentions for coreference resolution before.

We use a family of multilingual *T5* models (Xue et al., 2021), namely *mT5-base* and *mT5-large* with 580M and 1.2B parameters, respectively. We omit the demonstrations in our prompt, as they can make the input quite lengthy, and are unlikely to work with relatively small models. Instead, we use a prefix consisting of five tunable embeddings prepended to our input. This method was first presented by Li and Liang (2021). For all our experiments we employ the Openprompt library (Ding et al., 2022), which we locally extend so that it works with multilingual *T5* models.

Our task is formulated as follows. Given an input string consisting of one sentence, the desired output should include all mentions contained in the given sentence together with their start and end indices in brackets. Generated mentions should be separated from each other with a delimiter (a vertical bar). To help the model generate indices, we modify the input by adding the corresponding index to each token, like Kalyanpur et al. (2020) do. Example 5.1 shows the approach. Both the model and the input embeddings stay frozen, and only prefix embeddings, which are added to the input under the hood, get updated during the prompt training. The prompt itself is given in Example 5.2.

Example 5.1. Model input and output
Input: *0 já 1 Jsem 2 prý 3 v 4 USA 5 a 6 hry 7 skončily 8 , 9 uvedl 10 de 11 Merode 12 .*
Output: *já (0-0) | de Merode (10-11) | hry (6-6) | v USA (3-4)*

Example 5.2. Prompt
0 já 1 Jsem 2 prý 3 v 4 USA 5 a 6 hry 7 skončily 8 , 9 uvedl 10 de 11 Merode 12 . Find all valid mentions: [MASK]

The total number of training and development examples makes up 178,028 and 24,404 sentences, respectively. Sentences without mentions are omitted. As discontinuous mentions represent only a tiny portion of all the mentions, we omit them as well. We set the maximum input length to 256 tokens, and expect the generated output also to be no longer than that. The training is done on one NVIDIA GeForce GTX TITAN X GPU with 12 GB memory on all the available multilingual training data for five epochs with the batch size 1, the *AdamW* optimizer, learning rate of 5e-5 and a linear schedule with warm-up. It takes about a week to complete the training.

As we do not have access to the gold test data, we evaluate our mention generation approach on the development partition. The results in terms of recall, precision and F1 are presented in Table 2. The table also includes mention detection scores achieved by the baseline. We see that the baseline results are more than +10 points higher on the combined data, with our approach showing better F1 only for the *de_parcorfull* and *tr_itcc* corpora. However, baseline scores are not directly compa-

[3]We consider the version trained on all the available multilingual train data in CorefUD 1.1 with singletons excluded from evaluation.

rable with the scores reached using the prompting approach. To calculate the baseline's scores we use the predicted clusters with all singleton clusters removed. To be fair, we also exclude all gold singleton clusters from the evaluation. In contrast to that, our mention generation is done before coreference resolution. Thus, it is impossible to remove any singletons, as no clusters exist yet.

Table 2 shows that our method allows to get decent results, with *mT5-large* typically producing much better scores than *mT5-base*. As expected, better scores are normally achieved for larger datasets. However, there are some exceptions, e.g., the F1 score is 72.92 for *de_potsdamcc* and only 62.46 for *cs_pdt*, which have 4,061 and 142,951 continuous mentions in the training data, respectively. This points at the fact that some datasets contain "easier" mentions than others. Interestingly, the precision is always higher than recall, except for two *parcorfull* corpora. This may be an indication that the definition of a mention used to annotate them differs a lot from those applied to other datasets.

To better understand the results and find some possible space for improvement, we analysed the mistakes made by our approach. First, as expected, we discovered that shorter mentions in shorter sentences are more likely to be generated correctly - the average length of correctly generated and missing (not generated) mentions makes 2.03 and 5.86 tokens, respectively. The average length of sentences in which all mentions were identified correctly is about 11.67 tokens, while the sentences in which at least one mention was generated incorrectly (either a mention itself, or its indices, or both) contain 23.41 tokens on average. Second, among 21,133 wrong outputs (a) 379 (1.79%) do not have brackets with indices, and only four instances among them are correct mention strings; (b) 752 (3.56%) have a wrong delimiter, thus representing merged outputs, of which only 29 are fully correct, five are correct but have wrong indices, and 544 are wrong mentions with correct indices. Example B.1 in the Appendix B illustrates the problem. As for the rest 20,002 wrong outputs (i.e. cases consisting of one mention and one index pair), we found out that 245 (1.22%) of them have wrong indices, and 5,690 (28.45%) - wrong mention strings. Other 14,067 (70.33%) outputs have both wrong mentions and wrong indices. Finally, we detected that the average length of outputs with correct indices but wrong strings varies from 10.85 to 13.03 tokens, which shows that the model is still capable to deal with longer mentions. More information on that can be found in Appendix B.

Based on the error analysis, we would suggest the following modifications of the approach. First, simplification of the desired output seems to be promising. Our current output pattern is quite challenging, instead, we can ask the model to produce only the indices of mentions, like *'10-11'*, or a direct substring of the input string, like *'10 de 11 Merode'*. This would probably help to deal with missing spaces before punctuation marks, which make a large part of all mistakes. Next, we believe that training the prompt for more epochs, as well as tuning some other hyperparameters, like the number of prefix tokens, may lead to performance improvements. Experiments with other types of templates and a better prompt engineering may also be beneficial. Finally, it is possible to group the datasets depending on the mention definitions, train several prompts, and do prompt ensembling.

5.2 Coreference resolution

As we have a separate module to identify the mentions, we slightly change the baseline so that it performs only coreference resolution. This means that the model does not need to create spans, assign scores to them and do the pruning, because the mentions are already known. We re-train the baseline on gold mentions (including singletons) with all the default hyperparameters, and then evaluate it on mentions generated with our prefix prompt. While the original baseline reaches 66.78 CoNLL score on the combined development data, adding our prompt-based module to it causes about -7 points drop in performance. This is not unexpected, as mention identification results achieved by our method were in general worse than those produced by the baseline. Only for three datasets the CoNLL scores were higher, and for two out of these three our approach also demonstrated better mention identification results in comparison with the baseline. All scores can be found in Table 9 in the Appendix B. On average, according to the official leaderboard, our model reaches the CoNLL scores of 57.22 and 53.76 on the development and test data, respectively. In both cases it takes the last place on the list of eight (development) and ten (test) submissions. Still, we find the scores decent, considering how little effort our method takes.

Data	num	mT5-base			mT5-large			baseline
	men	R	P	F1	R	P	F1	F1
all	108,006	55.42	72.56	62.84	63.53	75.80	69.13	**79.90**
ca_ancora	7,280	46.11	67.48	54.79	54.52	71.23	61.77	**81.55**
cs_pcedt	23,784	56.90	67.16	61.61	63.23	71.13	66.95	**80.90**
cs_pdt	20,955	47.79	71.34	57.24	54.12	73.83	62.46	**78.76**
en_gum	5,508	61.86	80.54	69.97	71.10	81.98	76.15	**80.24**
en_parcorfull	79	69.62	27.36	39.29	70.89	25.34	37.33	**58.13**
fr_democrat	7,032	61.52	78.21	68.87	72.16	80.01	75.88	**78.63**
de_parcorfull	93	65.59	44.20	52.81	72.04	44.67	**55.14**	53.89
de_potsdamcc	558	56.99	70.20	62.91	69.00	77.31	72.92	**73.47**
hu_korkor	448	47.54	66.15	55.32	54.91	68.72	61.04	**70.85**
hu_szegedkoref	1,458	54.87	61.73	58.10	60.84	66.10	63.36	**68.23**
lt_lcc	366	48.09	55.17	53.39	55.46	63.04	59.01	**77.06**
no_bokmaal	6,446	65.54	80.80	72.38	76.79	85.23	80.79	**84.07**
no_nynorsk	5,193	67.24	79.76	72.97	77.89	83.83	80.75	**85.16**
pl_pcc	18,857	56.77	75.88	64.95	66.27	79.03	72.09	**77.49**
ru_rucor	2,297	68.35	78.70	73.16	75.49	80.61	77.97	**83.43**
es_ancora	7,161	46.64	66.91	54.97	54.11	71.83	61.72	**82.56**
tr_itcc	491	58.45	75.13	65.75	65.38	76.98	**70.70**	54.65

Table 2: Mention identification results. *All* stands for all the development data taken together (not the average).

6 Conclusion

In this paper we presented our systems for multilingual coreference resolution.

Our *DFKI-Adapt* submission leverages the existing data in different ways including joint pretraining, integrating adapters, adding character embeddings and loss-based re-training. It achieves 61.86 F1 on the official test set and 68.06 F1 on the development set. We provide a comparison of different settings for 12 languages from the CRAC shared task. Based on our analysis, joined pretraining with further fine-tuning on the respective dataset is the most beneficial setting per se but the largest gains can be achieved with the combination of different settings as implemented in the *DFKI-Adapt* system. Our experiments also show that while injecting the pre-trained adapter weights can be helpful for many languages, these pre-trained weights should not be further updated during training. In the future we would like to experiment more with the language-specific vs. task-specific adapters and test whether cross-lingual transfer via adapters could further improve the performance on the coreference resolution task.

Our second submission *DFKI-MPrompt* relies on a novel prompt-based approach for mention identification. It generates all possible mention strings together with their indices, given a sentence. Although the obtained scores were lower than baseline scores for the majority of the datasets, our method still has some potential. First, it can be improved by applying a better template, more optimal hyperparameters and a larger model. Second, it could be used as an additional tool helping span-based mention-ranking state-of-the-art models find mentions that are especially challenging for them, like split antecedents or discontinuous mentions. As a possible next step we plan experiments to check if our approach is capable of such a task.

Limitations

We believe that our *DFKI-Adapt* system could be further improved by adding more adapter weights and experimenting with the cross-lingual transfer learning. The current system uses adapters as a way of additional pre-training of the encoder but it would be interesting to see whether adapters for different languages can also benefit each other, similarly to the *combined_datasets* setting.

Casting mention identification as a prompt-based generation task also has its limitations. Using prompting, good results (sometimes even better than state-of-the-art) can be typically obtained with very large models that are not always freely available and require lots of computational resources. Even with relatively small models, like *T5*, prompt-tuning/inference may take several days, if one does not have access to powerful GPUs. This makes the process of finding the optimal prompt and hyperparameters very time-consuming.

Acknowledgements

The authors are supported by the German Ministry of Education and Research (BMBF): T. Anikina in project CORA4NLP (grant Nr. 01IW20010); N. Skachkova, A. Mokhova in IMPRESS (grant Nr. 01IS20076).

References

Monica Agrawal, Stefan Hegselmann, Hunter Lang, Yoon Kim, and David Sontag. 2022. Large language models are few-shot clinical information extractors. In *Proceedings of the 2022 Conference on Empirical Methods in Natural Language Processing*, pages 1998–2022, Abu Dhabi, United Arab Emirates. Association for Computational Linguistics.

Tatiana Anikina. 2023. Towards efficient dialogue processing in the emergency response domain. In *Proceedings of the 61st Annual Meeting of the Association for Computational Linguistics (Volume 4: Student Research Workshop)*, pages 212–225, Toronto, Canada. Association for Computational Linguistics.

Amit Bagga and Breck Baldwin. 1998. Algorithms for scoring coreference chains. In *Proceedings of the First International Conference on Language Resources and Evaluation Workshop on Linguistics Coreference*, volume 1, pages 563–566. Citeseer.

Tom Brown, Benjamin Mann, Nick Ryder, Melanie Subbiah, Jared D Kaplan, Prafulla Dhariwal, Arvind Neelakantan, Pranav Shyam, Girish Sastry, Amanda Askell, et al. 2020. Language models are few-shot learners. *Advances in neural information processing systems*, 33:1877–1901.

Agata Cybulska and Piek Vossen. 2014. Using a sledgehammer to crack a nut? Lexical diversity and event coreference resolution. In *Proceedings of the Ninth International Conference on Language Resources and Evaluation (LREC'14)*, pages 4545–4552, Reykjavik, Iceland. European Language Resources Association (ELRA).

Ning Ding, Shengding Hu, Weilin Zhao, Yulin Chen, Zhiyuan Liu, Haitao Zheng, and Maosong Sun. 2022. OpenPrompt: An open-source framework for prompt-learning. In *Proceedings of the 60th Annual Meeting of the Association for Computational Linguistics: System Demonstrations*, pages 105–113, Dublin, Ireland. Association for Computational Linguistics.

Wenxin Hou, Hanlin Zhu, Yidong Wang, Jindong Wang, Tao Qin, Renjun Xu, and Takahiro Shinozaki. 2021. Exploiting adapters for cross-lingual low-resource speech recognition. *IEEE/ACM Transactions on Audio, Speech, and Language Processing*, 30:317–329.

Neil Houlsby, Andrei Giurgiu, Stanislaw Jastrzebski, Bruna Morrone, Quentin De Laroussilhe, Andrea Gesmundo, Mona Attariyan, and Sylvain Gelly. 2019. Parameter-efficient transfer learning for NLP. In *Proceedings of International Conference on Machine Learning*, pages 2790–2799. PMLR.

Aditya Kalyanpur, Or Biran, Tom Breloff, Jennifer Chu-Carroll, Ariel Diertani, Owen Rambow, and Mark Sammons. 2020. Open-domain frame semantic parsing using Transformers.

Hamidreza Kobdani and Hinrich Schütze. 2010. Sucre: A modular system for coreference resolution. In *Proceedings of the 5th International Workshop on Semantic Evaluation*, pages 92–95.

Nghia T. Le, Fan Bai, and Alan Ritter. 2022. Few-shot anaphora resolution in scientific protocols via mixtures of in-context experts. In *Proceedings of Conference on Empirical Methods in Natural Language Processing*.

Jaeseong Lee, Seung-won Hwang, and Taesup Kim. 2022. FAD-X: Fusing adapters for cross-lingual transfer to low-resource languages. In *Proceedings of the 2nd Conference of the Asia-Pacific Chapter of the Association for Computational Linguistics and the 12th International Joint Conference on Natural Language Processing (Volume 2: Short Papers)*, pages 57–64, Online only. Association for Computational Linguistics.

Hector Levesque, Ernest Davis, and Leora Morgenstern. 2012. The Winograd schema challenge. In *Proceedings of the Thirteenth international conference on the principles of knowledge representation and reasoning*.

Xiang Lisa Li and Percy Liang. 2021. Prefix-tuning: Optimizing continuous prompts for generation. In *Proceedings of the 59th Annual Meeting of the Association for Computational Linguistics and the 11th International Joint Conference on Natural Language Processing (Volume 1: Long Papers)*, pages 4582–4597, Online. Association for Computational Linguistics.

Xi Victoria Lin, Todor Mihaylov, Mikel Artetxe, Tianlu Wang, Shuohui Chen, Daniel Simig, Myle Ott, Naman Goyal, Shruti Bhosale, Jingfei Du, Ramakanth Pasunuru, Sam Shleifer, Punit Singh Koura, Vishrav Chaudhary, Brian O'Horo, Jeff Wang, Luke Zettlemoyer, Zornitsa Kozareva, Mona Diab, Veselin Stoyanov, and Xian Li. 2022. Few-shot learning with multilingual generative language models. In *Proceedings of the 2022 Conference on Empirical Methods in Natural Language Processing*, pages 9019–9052, Abu Dhabi, United Arab Emirates. Association for Computational Linguistics.

Xiaoqiang Luo. 2005. On coreference resolution performance metrics. In *Proceedings of Human Language Technology Conference and Conference on Empirical Methods in Natural Language Processing*, pages 25–32.

Eleni Metheniti, Chloé Braud, Philippe Muller, and Laura Rivière. 2023. DisCut and DiscReT: MELODI at DISRPT 2023. In *Proceedings of the 3rd Shared Task on Discourse Relation Parsing and Treebanking (DISRPT 2023)*, pages 29–42, Toronto, Canada. The Association for Computational Linguistics.

Sewon Min, Mike Lewis, Luke Zettlemoyer, and Hannaneh Hajishirzi. 2022. MetaICL: Learning to learn in context. In *Proceedings of the 2022 Conference of the North American Chapter of the Association for Computational Linguistics: Human Language Technologies*, pages 2791–2809, Seattle, United States. Association for Computational Linguistics.

Anna Nedoluzhko, Michal Novák, Martin Popel, Zdeněk Žabokrtský, Amir Zeldes, and Daniel Zeman. 2022. CorefUD 1.0: Coreference meets Universal Dependencies. In *Proceedings of the Thirteenth Language Resources and Evaluation Conference*, pages 4859–4872.

Long Ouyang, Jeffrey Wu, Xu Jiang, Diogo Almeida, Carroll Wainwright, Pamela Mishkin, Chong Zhang, Sandhini Agarwal, Katarina Slama, Alex Ray, et al. 2022. Training language models to follow instructions with human feedback. *Advances in Neural Information Processing Systems*, 35:27730–27744.

Marinela Parovic, Goran Glavas, Ivan Vulic, and Anna Korhonen. 2022. BAD-X: Bilingual adapters improve zero-shot cross-lingual transfer. In *Proceedings of North American Chapter of the Association for Computational Linguistics*.

Ethan Perez, Douwe Kiela, and Kyunghyun Cho. 2021. True few-shot learning with language models. *Advances in neural information processing systems*, 34:11054–11070.

Sameer Pradhan, Alessandro Moschitti, Nianwen Xue, Olga Uryupina, and Yuchen Zhang. 2012. CoNLL-2012 shared task: Modeling multilingual unrestricted coreference in OntoNotes. In *Proceedings of Joint conference on EMNLP and CoNLL-shared task*, pages 1–40.

Sameer S. Pradhan, Eduard Hovy, Mitch Marcus, Martha Palmer, Lance Ramshaw, and Ralph Weischedel. 2007. OntoNotes: A unified relational semantic representation. In *Proceedings of International Conference on Semantic Computing (ICSC 2007)*, pages 517–526. IEEE.

Ondřej Pražák, Miloslav Konopík, and Jakub Sido. 2021. Multilingual coreference resolution with harmonized annotations. In *Proceedings of the International Conference on Recent Advances in Natural Language Processing (RANLP 2021)*, pages 1119–1123.

Alec Radford, Jeffrey Wu, Rewon Child, David Luan, Dario Amodei, Ilya Sutskever, et al. 2019. Language models are unsupervised multitask learners. *OpenAI blog*, 1(8):9.

Colin Raffel, Noam Shazeer, Adam Roberts, Katherine Lee, Sharan Narang, Michael Matena, Yanqi Zhou, Wei Li, and Peter J Liu. 2020. Exploring the limits of transfer learning with a unified text-to-text transformer. *The Journal of Machine Learning Research*, 21(1):5485–5551.

Sylvestre-Alvise Rebuffi, Hakan Bilen, and Andrea Vedaldi. 2017. Learning multiple visual domains with residual adapters. In *Advances in Neural Information Processing Systems*, volume 30. Curran Associates, Inc.

Marta Recasens and Eduard Hovy. 2011. BLANC: Implementing the rand index for coreference evaluation. *Natural language engineering*, 17(4):485–510.

Marta Recasens, Lluís Màrquez, Emili Sapena, M Antònia Martí, Mariona Taulé, Véronique Hoste, Massimo Poesio, and Yannick Versley. 2010. SemEval-2010 task 1: Coreference resolution in multiple languages. In *Proceedings of the 5th international workshop on semantic evaluation*, pages 1–8.

Sebastian Ruder, Ivan Vulić, and Anders Søgaard. 2022. Square one bias in NLP: Towards a multi-dimensional exploration of the research manifold. In *Findings of the Association for Computational Linguistics: ACL 2022*, pages 2340–2354, Dublin, Ireland. Association for Computational Linguistics.

Keisuke Sakaguchi, Ronan Le Bras, Chandra Bhagavatula, and Yejin Choi. 2021. Winogrande: An adversarial Winograd schema challenge at scale. *Communications of the ACM*, 64(9):99–106.

Gongbo Tang and Christian Hardmeier. 2023. Parallel data helps neural entity coreference resolution. In *Findings of the Association for Computational Linguistics: ACL 2023*, pages 3162–3171, Toronto, Canada. Association for Computational Linguistics.

Alexey Tikhonov and Max Ryabinin. 2021. It's All in the Heads: Using Attention Heads as a Baseline for Cross-Lingual Transfer in Commonsense Reasoning. In *Findings of the Association for Computational Linguistics: ACL-IJCNLP 2021*, pages 3534–3546, Online. Association for Computational Linguistics.

Ashish Vaswani, Noam Shazeer, Niki Parmar, Jakob Uszkoreit, Llion Jones, Aidan N Gomez, Ł ukasz Kaiser, and Illia Polosukhin. 2017. Attention is all you need. In *Advances in Neural Information Processing Systems*, volume 30. Curran Associates, Inc.

Marc Vilain, John D Burger, John Aberdeen, Dennis Connolly, and Lynette Hirschman. 1995. A model-theoretic coreference scoring scheme. In *Sixth Message Understanding Conference (MUC-6): Proceedings of a Conference Held in Columbia, Maryland, November 6-8, 1995.*

Linting Xue, Noah Constant, Adam Roberts, Mihir Kale, Rami Al-Rfou, Aditya Siddhant, Aditya Barua, and Colin Raffel. 2021. mT5: A massively multilingual pre-trained text-to-text transformer. In *Proceedings of the 2021 Conference of the North American Chapter of the Association for Computational Linguistics: Human Language Technologies*, pages 483–498, Online. Association for Computational Linguistics.

Xiaohan Yang, Eduardo Peynetti, Vasco Meerman, and Chris Tanner. 2022. What GPT knows about who is who. In *Proceedings of the Third Workshop on Insights from Negative Results in NLP*, pages 75–81, Dublin, Ireland. Association for Computational Linguistics.

Zdeněk Žabokrtský, Miloslav Konopík, Anna Nedoluzhko, Michal Novák, Maciej Ogrodniczuk, Martin Popel, Ondřej Pražák, Jakub Sido, and Daniel Zeman. 2023. Findings of the second shared task on multilingual coreference resolution. In *Proceedings of the Sixth Workshop on Computational Models of Reference, Anaphora and Coreference (CRAC 2023)*, pages 1–18.

Zdeněk Žabokrtský, Miloslav Konopík, Anna Nedoluzhko, Michal Novák, Maciej Ogrodniczuk, Martin Popel, Ondřej Pražák, Jakub Sido, Daniel Zeman, and Yilun Zhu. 2022. Findings of the shared task on multilingual coreference resolution. In *Proceedings of the CRAC 2022 Shared Task on Multilingual Coreference Resolution*, pages 1–17, Gyeongju, Republic of Korea. Association for Computational Linguistics.

Desislava Zhekova and Sandra Kübler. 2010. UBIU: A language-independent system for coreference resolution. In *Proceedings of the 5th International Workshop on Semantic Evaluation*, pages 96–99.

A DFKI-Adapt vs. other configurations

Tables 3-6 present the evaluation results on the development data for 12 languages. The CoNLL score is compared with the scores achieved by separate metrics, namely MUC, B^3 and CEAFE.

B Mention generation

B.1 Data statistics

Tables 7 and 8 present the main statistical facts about the CorefUD 1.1 data that help explain mention identification results. Table 7 illustrates the differences between the datasets in terms of size by providing information about the number of documents, sentences and tokens in the training and development partitions of separate corpora.

Table 8 gives for each dataset information about sentence lengths, number of continuous and discontinuous mentions, average number of mentions in a sentence, and average mention lengths. We see that the sentences in CorefUD 1.1 may be of different length and contain different number of mentions. On average, a sentence consists of 21 tokens, the shortest sentences (14.93 tokens on average) can be found in the *tr_itcc* dataset, and the longest (34.06 tokens on average) - in *es_ancora*. The total number of continuous and discontinuous mentions in all the training data makes up 794,643 and 5,543, respectively. Typically, a sentence includes 4.46 mentions, and the number of mentions in a sentence correlates with its length, e.g., in *es_ancora* a sentence contains 5.32 mentions on average, and in *tr_itcc* - only 1.80 mentions. Some sentences do not contain any mentions. Normally, a mention consists of 3.32 tokens, the longest mentions (4.98 tokens on average) occur in *es_ancora*, the shortest (1.53 tokens on average) - in the *lt_lcc* dataset.

B.2 Coreference resolution results

Table 9 presents coreference resolution results for all the development partitions of separate datasets. Note that we also evaluate our approach on the combined data (*all*). In contrast to this, the official leaderboard shows the averaged score based on separate results. Table 9 shows precision, recall and F1 (CoNLL) score produced by two versions of the baseline model. The *predicted mentions* section contains the results achieved by the original baseline trained on all the available training data. The *gold mentions* part - the points produced by baseline trained on all the gold mentions, given gold development mentions. Finally, the *generated mentions* section shows the scores reached by the baseline trained on the gold mentions when evaluated on the mentions generated by our mention identification module.

B.3 Mention generation errors

Example B.1 shows a typical error case. First, the generated mentions can not be separated, because the delimiter "|," is wrong. Second, one of the two gold mentions, namely *", fundador de la aerolínea Spantax"* starts with a comma, which the model fails to generate. However, despite the missing comma, the indices *(4-9)* corresponding to this mention are generated correctly.

Example B.1. Generated merged output
'Rodolfo Bay Wright, fundador de la aerolínea Spantax (1-9) |*, fundador de la aerolínea Spantax (4-9)'*
Gold output
'Rodolfo Bay Wright, fundador de la aerolínea Spantax (1-9) | *, fundador de la aerolínea Spantax (4-9)'*

We additionally analysed cases where the generated mention strings were wrong but the indices correct. It turned out that *mT5* tends to skip spaces before punctuation marks, while gold mentions have them, e.g., the model generates *'Eugene, Oregon'* instead of *'Eugene , Oregon'*. Moreover, we found out that many mentions in the gold data may start and/or end with a comma, like *', Juan José Ibarretxe ,'*, which was obviously confusing for the model.

Setting	es_ancora				de_potsdamcc				tr_itcc			
	MUC	B^3	$CEAFE$	$CoNLL$	MUC	B^3	$CEAFE$	$CoNLL$	MUC	B^3	$CEAFE$	$CoNLL$
mbert-joined	74.65	67.03	66.20	67.00	69.06	64.22	64.02	65.77	41.91	23.76	29.32	31.66
mbert-separate	71.87	64.14	63.09	66.37	63.52	58.03	55.22	58.92	41.48	22.64	29.94	31.35
char-embedding	73.42	66.03	64.52	67.99	61.98	54.88	48.63	55.16	26.89	10.83	16.20	17.98
joined-pre-training	74.97	68.00	66.50	**69.82**	66.67	59.99	59.44	62.03	43.30	21.06	28.03	30.80
combined-datasets	72.37	64.69	62.85	66.64	71.72	65.67	63.99	**67.12**	45.14	25.23	31.26	**33.88**
loss-re-training	71.87	64.34	62.67	66.29	64.98	58.03	56.28	59.77	36.28	15.87	17.68	23.28
task-adapters-frozen	72.67	64.90	63.38	66.99	67.08	62.14	63.63	64.28	30.47	12.38	19.20	20.68
task-adapters-tuned	68.69	60.28	58.61	62.53	65.02	57.45	58.33	60.27	7.51	3.79	9.45	6.91
DFKI-Adapt	75.26	68.21	66.74	**70.07**	72.99	67.46	67.40	**69.29**	50.64	29.69	33.06	**37.80**
CRAC-baseline	-	-	-	67.00	-	-	-	56.07	-	-	-	16.15

Table 3: Coreference resolution results on the development data for Spanish, German and Turkish

Setting	pl_pcc				cs_pdt				hu_szegedkoref			
	MUC	B^3	$CEAFE$	$CoNLL$	MUC	B^3	$CEAFE$	$CoNLL$	MUC	B^3	$CEAFE$	$CoNLL$
mbert-joined	72.44	63.48	60.30	65.41	71.21	64.12	63.72	66.35	61.91	57.62	59.80	59.78
mbert-separate	71.38	61.60	57.93	63.64	70.76	63.50	61.63	65.30	62.56	57.81	59.56	59.98
char-embedding	72.77	63.23	59.97	65.32	72.31	65.53	64.52	67.45	61.57	57.36	59.67	59.53
joined-pre-training	73.63	64.28	61.25	**66.38**	73.11	66.59	65.26	**68.32**	64.43	60.14	62.29	**62.29**
combined-datasets	73.31	64.09	61.24	**66.21**	71.86	64.75	63.25	66.62	62.55	57.91	60.78	60.42
loss-re-training	71.33	61.64	58.26	63.74	70.80	63.50	61.78	65.36	62.43	57.79	60.17	60.13
task-adapters-frozen	71.47	61.89	59.53	64.30	71.58	64.44	63.04	66.35	59.36	54.49	58.31	57.39
task-adapters-tuned	67.75	57.12	53.45	59.44	66.76	58.92	57.86	61.18	55.37	51.15	54.59	53.70
DFKI-Adapt	73.20	63.63	60.86	65.89	73.33	66.78	65.68	**68.60**	65.49	60.37	61.95	**62.60**
CRAC-baseline	-	-	-	64.17	-	-	-	65.66	-	-	-	58.96

Table 4: Coreference resolution results on the development data for Polish, Czech and Hungarian

Setting	ca_ancora				fr_democrat				en_gum			
	MUC	B^3	$CEAFE$	$CoNLL$	MUC	B^3	$CEAFE$	$CoNLL$	MUC	B^3	$CEAFE$	$CoNLL$
mbert-joined	74.30	65.87	66.74	**68.97**	71.41	51.74	56.05	59.74	77.66	63.28	56.45	**65.80**
mbert-separate	71.20	62.06	61.93	65.06	69.95	50.11	56.50	58.85	65.91	49.89	40.22	52.01
char-embedding	72.47	63.58	63.62	66.56	69.72	50.37	56.55	58.88	67.64	52.05	42.46	54.05
joined-pre-training	74.23	65.89	66.05	**68.72**	72.06	52.32	58.54	60.97	74.72	61.68	50.82	62.41
combined-datasets	72.27	63.30	63.31	66.29	72.43	52.27	58.56	**61.09**	42.01	32.46	31.27	35.25
loss-re-training	71.63	62.48	62.66	65.59	69.60	49.37	54.45	57.81	65.56	50.11	38.47	51.38
task-adapters-frozen	71.96	63.21	63.40	66.19	69.41	48.82	55.41	57.88	65.27	49.97	39.24	51.49
task-adapters-tuned	68.70	58.70	58.57	61.99	65.17	43.29	49.04	52.50	60.51	44.99	37.12	47.54
DFKI-Adapt	74.01	65.45	65.56	68.34	72.74	54.47	59.80	**62.34**	80.43	68.38	60.08	**69.63**
CRAC-baseline	-	-	-	65.60	-	-	-	57.22	-	-	-	66.87

Table 5: Coreference resolution results on the development data for Catalan, French and English

Setting	lt_lcc				ru_rucor				no_bokmaal			
	MUC	B^3	$CEAFE$	$CoNLL$	MUC	B^3	$CEAFE$	$CoNLL$	MUC	B^3	$CEAFE$	$CoNLL$
mbert-joined	73.44	69.55	70.68	71.22	74.63	54.16	57.46	62.08	80.10	66.54	62.79	69.81
mbert-separate	69.92	66.49	70.86	69.09	73.83	55.23	57.27	62.11	77.07	67.31	61.04	68.47
char-embedding	71.08	66.91	70.66	69.55	75.24	56.65	59.64	63.84	78.00	67.33	61.99	69.11
joined-pre-training	75.49	71.88	72.17	**73.18**	77.28	59.43	62.92	**66.54**	81.32	71.09	64.36	**72.26**
combined-datasets	77.33	73.85	76.12	**75.76**	75.58	57.23	60.93	64.58	78.19	67.80	61.28	69.09
loss-re-training	71.25	67.59	69.58	69.47	74.60	55.91	59.27	63.26	76.92	66.26	59.76	67.65
task-adapters-frozen	70.97	66.82	66.37	68.05	73.52	54.46	57.20	61.73	77.81	66.85	61.83	68.83
task-adapters-tuned	66.92	62.62	65.32	64.95	69.18	51.08	53.65	57.97	74.46	62.70	56.44	64.53
DFKI-Adapt	74.79	71.39	73.06	73.08	78.77	60.32	63.40	**67.50**	81.39	70.95	65.01	**72.45**
CRAC-baseline	-	-	-	66.96	-	-	-	63.04	-	-	-	58.44

Table 6: Coreference resolution results on the development data for Lithuanian, Russian and Norwegian

Data	train			dev		
	#doc	#sent	#tok	#doc	#sent	#tok
all	9,595	194,460	3,899,182	1,325	26,698	547,869
ca_ancora	1,011	10,638	337,876	131	1,443	49,695
cs_pcedt	1,875	39,832	964,606	337	6,960	169,211
cs_pdt	2,533	38,725	670,889	316	5,228	90,645
en_gum	151	8,548	147,949	22	1,117	19,654
en_parcorfull	15	457	8,765	2	48	1,155
fr_democrat	50	10,382	228,100	46	1,192	28,279
de_parcorfull	15	457	8,649	2	48	1,098
de_potsdamcc	142	1,817	26,677	17	216	3,376
hu_korkor	76	1,086	21,063	9	130	2,715
hu_szegedkoref	320	7,138	104,428	40	846	12,355
lt_lcc	80	1,330	30,082	10	213	3,385
no_bokmaal	284	13,071	203,220	31	1,317	21,658
no_nynorsk	336	10,320	172,764	28	1,158	17,977
pl_pcc	1,463	28,722	431,999	183	3,573	53,999
ru_rucor	145	7,969	123,599	18	1,286	21,139
es_ancora	1,080	11,336	373,402	131	1,367	46,668
tr_itcc	19	3,532	45,114	2	556	4,860

Table 7: Number of documents, sentences and tokens in CorefUD 1.1

Data	Sent len			num	num	# cont in sent			men
	max	min	avg	cont	disc	max	min	avg	len
all	405	1	21.00	794,643	5,543	156	0	4.46	3.32
ca_ancora	239	2	32.61	48,705	1	27	1	4.81	4.94
cs_pcedt	134	1	25.27	138,713	1,044	22	0	3.85	3.83
cs_pdt	195	1	18.25	142,951	1,958	25	0	3.99	3.22
en_gum	110	1	18.32	41,649	0	40	1	5.21	3.05
en_parcorfull	58	4	20.09	717	5	11	0	2.13	2.02
fr_democrat	125	1	22.34	63,562	0	40	1	6.25	2.37
de_parcorfull	60	4	20.67	749	2	11	1	2.33	1.94
de_potsdamcc	54	2	16.35	4,061	265	13	0	2.72	2.76
hu_korkor	79	5	19.85	3,167	19	16	0	3.12	2.46
hu_szegedkoref	123	2	15.89	12,555	45	19	0	2.23	1.75
lt_lcc	88	2	23.56	3,723	0	15	1	3.09	1.53
no_bokmaal	88	1	15.86	61,183	339	28	0	4.80	2.94
no_nynorsk	120	1	16.97	51,450	211	34	1	5.07	3.10
pl_pcc	405	1	15.46	149,057	1,618	156	0	5.38	2.87
ru_rucor	129	1	20.24	12,576	36	34	0	2.47	1.64
es_ancora	119	2	34.06	57,223	0	23	1	5.32	4.98
tr_itcc	82	2	14.93	2,602	0	11	1	1.80	1.94

Table 8: Sentence and mention properties in training data

Data	predicted mentions			gold mentions			generated mentions		
	R	P	F1 (CoNLL)	R	P	F1 (CoNLL)	R	P	F1 (CoNLL)
all	61.14	73.73	66.78	75.05	82.22	78.42	50.56	72.76	59.58
ca_ancora	62.92	75.76	68.72	78.13	85.35	81.57	45.08	73.11	55.73
cs_pcedt	62.65	74.50	68.01	78.53	87.17	82.59	54.52	75.62	63.32
cs_pdt	58.64	75.91	66.10	74.38	81.43	77.70	44.63	74.52	55.76
en_gum	58.55	73.27	65.02	70.70	76.60	73.45	53.92	72.17	61.55
en_parcorful	65.61	38.18	48.16	90.98	91.96	91.05	65.23	35.38	45.54
fr_democrat	57.99	65.32	60.89	66.19	69.74	67.20	52.72	62.82	56.53
de_parcorfull	42.06	35.15	38.17	91.13	92.82	91.90	67.48	52.76	*58.86*
de_potsdamcc	58.81	70.72	64.16	71.65	82.51	76.56	65.02	68.25	*66.38*
hu_korkor	47.73	65.38	55.11	68.26	75.13	71.45	38.88	56.64	46.06
hu_szegedkoref	56.11	65.34	60.34	80.57	85.86	83.12	47.13	59.82	52.71
lt_lcc	65.85	80.70	72.47	89.84	92.72	91.17	55.10	73.40	62.94
no_bokmaal	66.83	76.47	71.13	69.73	77.20	72.97	60.24	74.30	66.16
no_nynorsk	67.93	75.28	71.07	70.58	76.58	73.10	63.56	74.39	68.18
pl_pcc	61.39	70.63	65.64	70.84	77.22	72.43	52.99	68.75	59.79
ru_rucor	60.91	67.73	63.26	69.07	80.78	73.81	52.18	69.33	58.92
es_ancora	62.80	77.36	69.31	76.86	86.18	81.25	46.14	76.06	57.41
tr_itcc	27.91	40.70	30.82	59.03	68.74	61.47	30.30	51.98	*36.84*

Table 9: Baseline's coreference resolution results on the development data

Neural End-to-End Coreference Resolution using Morphological Information

Tuğba Pamay Arslan* and **Kutay Acar†** and **Gülşen Eryiğit***
İTÜ NLP Research Group
Department of [AI&Data*, Computer†] Engineering
Faculty of Computer&Informatics
Istanbul Technical University
[*pamay, †acarku18, *gulsen.cebiroglu]@itu.edu.tr

Abstract

In morphologically rich languages, words consist of morphemes containing deeper information in morphology, and thus such languages may necessitate the use of morpheme-level representations as well as word representations. This study introduces a neural multilingual end-to-end coreference resolution system by incorporating morphological information in transformer-based word embeddings on the baseline model. This proposed model participated in the Sixth Workshop on Computational Models of Reference, Anaphora and Coreference (CRAC 2023). Including morphological information explicitly into the coreference resolution improves the performance, especially in morphologically rich languages (e.g., Catalan, Hungarian, and Turkish). The introduced model outperforms the baseline system by 2.57 percentage points on average by obtaining 59.53% CoNLL F-score.

1 Introduction

Coreference Resolution (CR) is the task of determining coreferential relations between mentions referring to the same real-world entity in a document. CR is one of the essential components of comprehending natural language and is investigated under the semantic level of natural language processing (NLP). An end-to-end CR system consists of two stages which are trained jointly: 1) Mention detection and 2) Coreference linking. In the first, all possibly referential mentions are extracted in a text. Then, the coreferential relations between the automatically predicted mentions are created during the linking stage. When the CR task crosses with the complex linguistic diversity of natural languages, it becomes even more difficult, and morphological richness is one of such diversity. Morphologically rich languages require considering sub-word units (or morphemes) which carry deeper information at the morphology level. Therefore, this study explores the impact of including morphology information explicitly in a neural multilingual end-to-end CR system. Moreover, even if CR is an actively studied topic for quite a long time, the multilingual studies are currently in the process of development. Most studies propose CR datasets in their own data format and report their performances in one language only. The lack of quality and standardized datasets makes building multilingual CR systems harder. CorefUD initiative fills this gap in the CR literature by proposing a universal coreference representation scheme which was built on top of the Universal Dependencies (Nivre et al., 2017, 2020; Grobol and Tyers, 2023) initiative.

In this paper, we propose a neural, multilingual, end-to-end CR model trained with the data convened in CorefUD v1.1 (Novák et al., 2022); we extend the baseline model (Pražák et al., 2021) by enhancing the transformer-based word embeddings with dense and sparse (i.e., one/multi-hot encoding) vector representations of morphological information (i.e., POS tags and morphological features). The CorefUD v1.1 contains 17 different datasets for twelve languages in a harmonized, universal scheme. The proposed CR model employing sparse vector representations of morphological information achieves 59.53% CoNLL score on the test set (average across all languages), which means a 2.57 percentage points improvement over the baseline. The results show that the impact of explicitly incorporated morphological information is particularly high in the CR performance of morphologically rich languages. The paper is structured as follows: Section 2 gives the related work, Section 3 introduces the proposed neural model in detail, Section 4 presents the experimental setup and results, and Section 5 gives the conclusion.

2 Related Work

Deep learning-based CR approaches conforming to the end-to-end fashion have begun to be studied extensively in the last few years. Lee et al. (2017) proposes the first end-to-end neural CR system,

Proceedings of the CRAC 2023 Shared Task on Multilingual Coreference Resolution, pages 34–40
December 7, 2023

which creates a base for later studies. This study is enhanced with transformer-based embeddings via BERT (Kantor and Globerson, 2019) and Span-BERT (Joshi et al., 2020) with the higher-order inference (HOI) mechanism on top which are featured by Lee et al. (2018). Moreover, Liu et al. (2020) proposes a neural CR system employing entity-based features which were obtained by graph neural networks. In parallel, Park et al. (2020) introduce BERT-SRU-based Pointer Networks with the integration of morpheme boundaries as features for Korean. There are many studies proposed in the previous multilingual CR shared task (CRAC 2022) (Žabokrtský et al., 2022). The winning team of the shared task was ÚFAL CorPipe with 2 of their 3 submissions being on the leaderboard. The best model, *straka*, is trained jointly on all training data in all languages, and provides 70.72% CoNLL F-score by primary metric. *ondfa* (Pražák et al., 2021) is a baseline-based model using pre-trained XLM-RobertaLarge (Conneau et al., 2019) and also containing mention-head prediction. With the power of the mention-head prediction component, the model ends up getting a higher head-match score. *K-Sap* (Saputa, 2022) is introduced for only Polish. In addition to neural CR systems, rule-based models (*berulasek*, *simple-rule-based*, *Moravec*) also exist in the CRAC 2022.

Available annotated CR datasets in the literature are in a lack of standardization, which makes the development of multilingual CR systems complicated. By means of the CorefUD scheme (Novák et al., 2022), a multilingual coreference dataset collection is established and the task is shaped into a more generalized form. In parallel, CRAC organizations encourage researchers to develop and submit their own systems utilizing CorefUD dataset under the shared representation. CRAC 2022 was organized with the CorefUD v1.0 (Nedoluzhko et al., 2022) containing 13 datasets for 10 languages. CRAC 23 is organized with CorefUD v1.1 release. This version consists of 17 different datasets for 12 languages. Recent contributions involve Hungarian with one dataset, Turkish with one dataset, and Norwegian with two datasets. These made Turkish and Norwegian to appear in the CorefUD collection for the first time.

3 The Proposed Model

The introduced model is a modified version of the baseline model provided in the CRAC 2023 Shared Task (Žabokrtský et al., 2023), with the span representations updated. The baseline model (Pražák et al., 2021) provides a multilingual, end-to-end neural CR system which is a re-implementation of an available study (Xu and Choi, 2020). Basically, the model learns the probability distribution of coreferential links in the training data by maximizing the marginalized log-likelihood of gold antecedents for each possible span. To rank automatically detected referential mentions and link them with their possible antecedents, the model estimates the combination of two types of scores: 1) individual mention score, and 2) paired antecedent score. Individual mention score represents the likelihood of a span being a referential mention. Antecedent score entails a span pair and ranks their possibility of being coreferent. Since spans are considered as a sequence of words, they are represented by their words' embeddings obtained from a transformer, i.e., BERT.

This study introduces an enhanced span representation by incorporating morphological information explicitly in addition to contextual embeddings obtained by BERT. Each span embedding consists of three main sub-parts[1]: the embeddings of its first and last tokens, and the head attended embeddings of all tokens, as formularized in Equation (1) in the baseline model. In the equation, s_i represents the ith span, and $e(s_i)$ indicates the embedding of the related span.

$$e(s_i) = e(s_{i_{first}}) \oplus e(s_{i_{last}}) \oplus e(s_{i_{head}}) \qquad (1)$$

This study extends the first and last tokens' embeddings by incorporating one/multi-hot encoded morphological information explicitly. There are two types of morphological information utilized: universal part-of-speech (UPOS) and universal morphological features (Feats). The output sample of this procedure is shown for the first token's embedding in the Equation (2). The operation annotated by $\oplus$ is concatenation. Therefore the size of $e(s_i)$ is extended by the total unique number of universal POS tags and morphological features in the CorefUD collection. The same procedure is also applied to the last token's embedding.

$$\begin{aligned} e(s_{i_{first}}) =& e(s_{i_{first}}[form]) \oplus \\ & enc(s_{i_{first}}[upos]) \oplus \\ & enc(s_{i_{first}}[feats]) \end{aligned} \qquad (2)$$

[1]The span representation also contains various metadata (speaker, genre, span width) embeddings, and also embedded distance between a span and its antecedent. These secondary information are not formularized in equations to make them more readable.

4 Experimental Setup & Results

This section introduces the performance of the proposed model and also intermediate results.

4.1 Experimental Setup

The model utilizes a transformer-based neural language model, BERT[2] (Devlin et al., 2019), which is multilingual, base, and case sensitive. The model is trained using the default hyper-parameters, except maximum segment length being 256 instead of 512[3]. The hardware used in training is Tesla v100 graphic card. We trained our model for 24 epochs and the number of documents in the joint training data is 9595. The gradient update frequency is 1 so the total gradient update count is 230280 accordingly. The total time for training is 25-30 hours on average across the experiments.

Universal POS tags and morphological features are employed as morphological information in this study. One should note that, in the dataset, multiple morphological features are collected under the same information unit, separated by pipe symbols. Therefore, while one-hot encoding is suitable for POS tags, morphological features require multi-hot encoding, e.g., UPOS="NOUN" and FEATS="Case=Nom|Number=Plur" have upos_one_hot = [00100000...] (supposing NOUN is the third UPOS) and feats_multihot = [0100100...] (supposing Number=Plur is the second and Case=Nom the fifth feature). The total numbers of unique POS tags and morphological features are 20 and 210, respectively. Since morphological information is inserted to both the first and last tokens' embeddings, the dimensionality of the span embedding has increased by 460 for the one/multi-hot encoding technique.

In the case of dense vector representation, embedding layers with the dimensionality of 5 are deployed for POS tags and morphological features separately. To preserve the dimensionality, multiple morphological features are averaged out. All experiments are operated on a joined multilingual training set containing training data from all CorefUD languages. The only official evaluation criterion for the shared task is CoNLL, calculated as the macro-average F1 values of MUC (Vilain et al., 1995), B-cubed (Bagga and Baldwin, 1998) and CEAFe (Pradhan et al., 2014) scores of the predictions. The primary score is calculated using the head-match. That is, if the heads of a gold-standard and predicted mentions correspond to the same token, they are considered as a match. For that reason, the predicted mentions are reduced to their head tokens during the evaluation, with the help of `MoveHead` utility of Udapi[4] (Popel et al., 2017).

4.2 Results & Discussion

Several experiments were conducted to maximize the performance while enhancing span representations with morphological information. The results are given in Table 1. All contributions are made to the baseline model.

System	CoNLL
BASELINE	58.99
+{U,F}$_{emb}$	60.75
+{U}$_{enc}$	61.27
+{U,F}$_{enc}$ (morphbase)	**61.35**

Table 1: The performances of the intermediate and the proposed models evaluated on the development sets (CoNLL score in %).

While the first two rows below the *BASELINE* indicate the intermediate systems, the final system, named *morphbase* hereinafter, is the proposed model which participates in the CRAC 2023 shared task by our team, `TrCR`. As intermediate investigations, in Table 1, the models are named with the employed linguistic information; U indicates the use of universal POS tags and F indicates the use of morphological features. The results show all models exploiting morphological information surpass the performance of the baseline model by varying amounts.

We try to use both dense embeddings and one hot encodings for our morphological information representations; The first attempt is to utilize dense representations of both universal POS tags and morphological features, named {U,F}$_{emb}$. This model provides 60.75% CoNLL score which is 1.76 percentage points higher than the baseline. The second model, {U}$_{enc}$ uses a one-hot encoded version of only universal POS tags, and surpasses our first intermediate model by 0.52 percentage points. The model submitted to the shared task, {U,F}$_{enc}$ (named morphbase) employs encoded versions of both universal POS tags and morphological features. The *morphbase* model gives the best per-

[2]`https://huggingface.co/bert-base-multilingual-cased`

[3]`https://github.com/ondfa/coref-multiling/blob/master/experiments.conf`

[4]`https://github.com/udapi/udapi-python`

System	AVG	ca_ancora	cs_pcedt	cs_pdt	de_parcor	de_potsdam	en_gum	en_parcor	es_ancora	fr_democrat	hu_szeged	lt_lcc	pl_pcc	ru_rcr	hu_korkor	no_bokmaal	no_nynorsk	tr_itcc
BASELINE	58.99	65.60	65.72	65.66	**57.25**	56.07	**66.87**	**56.56**	67.00	57.22	58.96	66.96	64.17	**63.04**	48.38	58.44	68.78	16.15
morphbase	**61.35**	**68.85**	**67.97**	**66.05**	50.10	**63.51**	65.42	44.85	**69.98**	**59.77**	**59.19**	**72.74**	**65.61**	62.93	**53.25**	**71.02**	**69.15**	**32.63**
Diff	↑2.36	↑3.25	↑2.25	↑0.39	↓7.15	↑7.44	↓1.45	↓11.71	↑2.98	↑2.55	↑0.23	↑5.78	↑1.44	↓0.11	↑4.87	↑12.58	↑0.37	↑16.48

Table 2: Dev set results for individual languages in the primary metric (CoNLL).

System	AVG	ca_ancora	cs_pcedt	cs_pdt	de_parcor	de_potsdam	en_gum	en_parcor	es_ancora	fr_democrat	hu_szeged	lt_lcc	pl_pcc	ru_rcr	hu_korkor	no_bokmaal	no_nynorsk	tr_itcc
BASELINE	56.96	65.26	**67.72**	**65.22**	**44.11**	57.13	**63.08**	35.19	66.93	**55.31**	55.32	63.57	66.08	**69.03**	40.71	65.10	65.78	22.75
morphbase	**59.53**	**68.23**	64.89	64.74	39.96	**64.87**	62.80	**40.81**	**69.01**	53.18	**56.41**	**64.08**	**67.88**	68.53	**52.91**	**68.17**	**66.35**	**39.22**
Diff	↑2.57	↑2.97	↓2.83	↓0.48	↓4.15	↑7.74	↓0.28	↑5.62	↑2.08	↓2.13	↑1.09	↑0.51	↑1.8	↓0.5	↑12.2	↑3.07	↑0.57	↑16.47

Table 3: Test set results for individual languages in the primary metric (CoNLL).

formance among all investigated models with a 61.35% CoNLL score which is 2.36 percentage points higher than the baseline. The one/multi-hot encoding technique performs better in capturing sparse tag combinations, which may be one reason why models using this technique are more successful than the model using dense representations.

There were 10 submissions in this year's shared task, CRAC 2023. The winner model of this year, *CorPipe* (Straka and Straková, 2022) preserved their positions on the leaderboard in the previous shared task and provides 74.90% CoNLL scores on average. We are ranked at 7th place (Table 5) on the macro-averaged score, indicated as *morphbase* in Table 5. On individual dataset scores, our highest rank is on Catalan (ca_ancora), which is the 5th place. Then it is followed by 6th place on Turkish (tr_itcc), Hungarian (hu_korkor), German (de_potsdamcc), and English (en_parcorfull) datasets. Tables 2 and 3 present the performance of the *morphbase* model, in all languages with the primary metric. The top row lists the name of datasets for each language. The row 'Diff' indicates the improvement of the *morphbase* over the baseline model. Enhanced span representation achieves 61.35% and 59.53% CoNLL performance on average, which are higher than 2.36 and 2.57 percentage points on development and test sets, respectively. Including morphological information explicitly into the baseline model improves the performance of the following morphologically rich languages: Catalan, Czech, Hungarian, Spanish, French, Lithuanian, Polish, Norwegian, and Turkish, however, in Czech and French, improvements are only observed on the development sets.

The highest performance increment is on Turkish (tr_itcc) by 16.48 percentage points on the development set and 16.47 percentage points on the test set. Since Turkish possesses prominently rich morphology, such enhancement is not utterly surprising. For Hungarian, a significant increase is obtained on hu_korkor dataset by 4.87 percentage points on the development set and 12.2 percentage points on the test set. It is followed by Norwegian which exhibits agglutinative characteristics on verbal suffixes and the baseline model is surpassed by 12.58% percentage points on the development set. The performance of Spanish is improved by 2.98 and 2.08 percentage points compared to baseline by obtaining 69.98% and 69.01% CoNLL scores on development and test sets, orderly. While there is an undeniable drop in performance for German (de_parcorfull) and English (en_parcorfull) datasets, there is no such drop in the remaining datasets of these languages. The small sizes of these datasets (for details, check Table 4) might be the reason for such results. Moreover, it can be observed that in the languages having large datasets such as Czech, Spanish, and Polish, the effect of morphological information integration seems not as prominent as in medium-sized datasets.

5 Conclusion

This study proposed a neural, end-to-end, multilingual CR model which is an improved version of the baseline model incorporating morphological information into transformer-based span embeddings. The results show that extending word representations with morphological information helps CR systems on average but especially for languages with high morphological complexity and agglutinative characteristics (e.g., Catalan, Hungarian, Norwegian, and Turkish). The proposed model completed the CRAC 2023 shared task at 7th place on average. Besides, on individual dataset scores, our highest rank is on Catalan (ca_ancora), which is the 5th place. Then it is followed by 6th place on Turkish (tr_itcc), Hungarian (hu_korkor), German (de_potsdamcc), and English (en_parcorfull).

Limitations

The main limitation of this study is that the training is operated on the joined data including all languages and there are no language-specific adjustments to the model. Therefore, the model treats all data equally even if the language has specific characteristics which might be useful to detect referential mentions and/or make coreferential relations between them. It is considered that it might increase the performance of particular languages having distinctive linguistic characteristics.

The proposed model is trained by only default hyper-parameters with the baseline model, that is, no hyper-parameter tuning could be done due to the time and resource constraints. The introduced model may need another set of parameters to perform better. For example, due to the hardware constraints, the transformer's segment size is used as 256, which is smaller than the usual, 512. The effect of such a constraint is most likely to be negative since it is a limiting factor when it comes to capturing the longer context.

Beyond the listed limitations, this study showed the positive impact of the interaction between transformer-based word representations and morphological information on the CR, despite the increasing popularity of deep learning, and the power of transformers. In future work, firstly, we plan to conduct error-analysis on languages which our model, morphbase, provided lower performances than the baseline model. We also plan to apply the proposed idea to other SOTA end-to-end neural multilingual CR systems. Moreover, we will work on increasing the performance of other languages by representing language-specific features in the model.

Acknowledgements

This work is funded by the Scientific and Technological Research Council of Turkey (TUBITAK) with a TUBITAK 2515 (European Cooperation in Science and Technology - COST) project Grant No. 123E079. Computing resources used in this work were provided by the National Center for High Performance Computing of Turkey (UHeM) under grant number 4015042023 and also by İTÜ Artificial Intelligence and Data Science Application and Research Center.

References

Amit Bagga and Breck Baldwin. 1998. Algorithms for scoring coreference chains. In *The first international conference on language resources and evaluation workshop on linguistics coreference*, volume 1, pages 563–566. Citeseer.

Alexis Conneau, Kartikay Khandelwal, Naman Goyal, Vishrav Chaudhary, Guillaume Wenzek, Francisco Guzmán, Edouard Grave, Myle Ott, Luke Zettlemoyer, and Veselin Stoyanov. 2019. Unsupervised cross-lingual representation learning at scale. *arXiv preprint arXiv:1911.02116*.

Jacob Devlin, Ming-Wei Chang, Kenton Lee, and Kristina Toutanova. 2019. BERT: Pre-training of deep bidirectional transformers for language understanding. In *Proceedings of the 2019 Conference of the North American Chapter of the Association for Computational Linguistics: Human Language Technologies, Volume 1 (Long and Short Papers)*, pages 4171–4186, Minneapolis, Minnesota. Association for Computational Linguistics.

Loïc Grobol and Francis Tyers, editors. 2023. *Proceedings of the Sixth Workshop on Universal Dependencies (UDW, GURT/SyntaxFest 2023)*. Association for Computational Linguistics, Washington, D.C.

Mandar Joshi, Danqi Chen, Yinhan Liu, Daniel S. Weld, Luke Zettlemoyer, and Omer Levy. 2020. SpanBERT: Improving pre-training by representing and predicting spans. *Transactions of the Association for Computational Linguistics*, 8:64–77.

Ben Kantor and Amir Globerson. 2019. Coreference resolution with entity equalization. In *Proceedings of the 57th Annual Meeting of the Association for Computational Linguistics*, pages 673–677, Florence, Italy. Association for Computational Linguistics.

Kenton Lee, Luheng He, Mike Lewis, and Luke Zettlemoyer. 2017. End-to-end neural coreference resolution. In *Proceedings of the 2017 Conference on Empirical Methods in Natural Language Processing*, pages 188–197, Copenhagen, Denmark. Association for Computational Linguistics.

Kenton Lee, Luheng He, and Luke Zettlemoyer. 2018. Higher-order coreference resolution with coarse-to-fine inference. In *Proceedings of the 2018 Conference of the North American Chapter of the Association for Computational Linguistics: Human Language Technologies, Volume 2 (Short Papers)*, pages

687–692, New Orleans, Louisiana. Association for Computational Linguistics.

Lu Liu, Zhenqiao Song, and Xiaoqing Zheng. 2020. Improving coreference resolution by leveraging entity-centric features with graph neural networks and second-order inference. *arXiv preprint arXiv:2009.04639*.

Anna Nedoluzhko, Michal Novák, Martin Popel, Zdeněk Žabokrtský, Amir Zeldes, and Daniel Zeman. 2022. CorefUD 1.0: Coreference meets Universal Dependencies. In *Proceedings of the Thirteenth Language Resources and Evaluation Conference*, pages 4859–4872, Marseille, France. European Language Resources Association.

Joakim Nivre, Marie-Catherine de Marneffe, Filip Ginter, Jan Hajič, Christopher D. Manning, Sampo Pyysalo, Sebastian Schuster, Francis Tyers, and Daniel Zeman. 2020. Universal Dependencies v2: An evergrowing multilingual treebank collection. In *Proceedings of the Twelfth Language Resources and Evaluation Conference*, pages 4034–4043, Marseille, France. European Language Resources Association.

Joakim Nivre, Daniel Zeman, Filip Ginter, and Francis Tyers. 2017. Universal Dependencies. In *Proceedings of the 15th Conference of the European Chapter of the Association for Computational Linguistics: Tutorial Abstracts*, Valencia, Spain. Association for Computational Linguistics.

Michal Novák, Martin Popel, Zdeněk Žabokrtský, Daniel Zeman, Anna Nedoluzhko, Kutay Acar, Peter Bourgonje, Silvie Cinková, Gülşen Cebiroğlu Eryiğit, Jan Hajič, Christian Hardmeier, Dag Haug, Tollef Jørgensen, Andre Kåsen, Pauline Krielke, Frédéric Landragin, Ekaterina Lapshinova-Koltunski, Petter Mæhlum, M.Antònia Martí, Marie Mikulová, Anders Nøklestad, Maciej Ogrodniczuk, Lilja Øvrelid, Tuğba Pamay Arslan, Marta Recasens, Per Erik Solberg, Manfred Stede, Milan Straka, Svetlana Toldova, Noémi Vadász, Erik Velldal, Veronika Vincze, Amir Zeldes, and Voldemaras Žitkus. 2022. Coreference in universal dependencies 1.1 (CorefUD 1.1). LINDAT/CLARIAH-CZ digital library at the Institute of Formal and Applied Linguistics (ÚFAL), Faculty of Mathematics and Physics, Charles University.

Cheoneum Park, Jamin Shin, Sungjoon Park, Joonho Lim, and Changki Lee. 2020. Fast end-to-end coreference resolution for Korean. In *Findings of the Association for Computational Linguistics: EMNLP 2020*, pages 2610–2624, Online. Association for Computational Linguistics.

Martin Popel, Zdeněk Žabokrtský, and Martin Vojtek. 2017. Udapi: Universal API for Universal Dependencies. In *Proceedings of the NoDaLiDa 2017 Workshop on Universal Dependencies (UDW 2017)*, pages 96–101, Gothenburg, Sweden. Association for Computational Linguistics.

Sameer Pradhan, Xiaoqiang Luo, Marta Recasens, Eduard Hovy, Vincent Ng, and Michael Strube. 2014. Scoring coreference partitions of predicted mentions: A reference implementation. In *Proceedings of the 52nd Annual Meeting of the Association for Computational Linguistics (Volume 2: Short Papers)*, pages 30–35, Baltimore, Maryland. Association for Computational Linguistics.

Ondřej Pražák, Miloslav Konopík, and Jakub Sido. 2021. Multilingual coreference resolution with harmonized annotations. In *Proceedings of the International Conference on Recent Advances in Natural Language Processing (RANLP 2021)*, pages 1119–1123.

Karol Saputa. 2022. Coreference resolution for Polish: Improvements within the CRAC 2022 shared task. In *Proceedings of the CRAC 2022 Shared Task on Multilingual Coreference Resolution*, pages 18–22, Gyeongju, Republic of Korea. Association for Computational Linguistics.

Milan Straka and Jana Straková. 2022. ÚFAL CorPipe at CRAC 2022: Effectivity of multilingual models for coreference resolution. In *Proceedings of the CRAC 2022 Shared Task on Multilingual Coreference Resolution*, pages 28–37, Gyeongju, Republic of Korea. Association for Computational Linguistics.

Marc Vilain, John Burger, John Aberdeen, Dennis Connolly, and Lynette Hirschman. 1995. A model-theoretic coreference scoring scheme. In *Sixth Message Understanding Conference (MUC-6): Proceedings of a Conference Held in Columbia, Maryland, November 6-8, 1995*.

Liyan Xu and Jinho D. Choi. 2020. Revealing the myth of higher-order inference in coreference resolution. In *Proceedings of the 2020 Conference on Empirical Methods in Natural Language Processing (EMNLP)*, pages 8527–8533, Online. Association for Computational Linguistics.

Zdeněk Žabokrtský, Miloslav Konopík, Anna Nedoluzhko, Michal Novák, Maciej Ogrodniczuk, Martin Popel, Ondřej Pražák, Jakub Sido, and Daniel Zeman. 2023. Findings of the Second Shared Task on Multilingual Coreference Resolution. In *Proceedings of the CRAC 2023 Shared Task on Multilingual Coreference Resolution*, pages 1–18, Singapore. Association for Computational Linguistics.

Zdeněk Žabokrtský, Miloslav Konopík, Anna Nedoluzhko, Michal Novák, Maciej Ogrodniczuk, Martin Popel, Ondřej Pražák, Jakub Sido, Daniel Zeman, and Yilun Zhu. 2022. Findings of the shared task on multilingual coreference resolution. In *Proceedings of the CRAC 2022 Shared Task on Multilingual Coreference Resolution*, pages 1–17, Gyeongju, Republic of Korea. Association for Computational Linguistics.

A Appendix

Stat	ca_ancora	cs_pcedt	cs_pdt	de_parcorfull	de_potsdamcc	en_gum	en_parcorfull	es_ancora	fr_democrat	hu_szegedkoref	lt_lcc	pl_pcc	ru_rucor	hu_korkor	no_bokmaalnarc	no_nynorsknarc	tr_itcc
docs	1,298	2,312	3,165	19	176	195	19	1,356	126	400	100	1,828	181	94	346	394	24
sents	13,613	49,208	49,428	543	2,238	10,761	543	14,159	13,057	8,820	1,714	35,784	9,035	1,351	15,742	12,481	4,733
words	435,690	1,191,599	857,109	10,602	33,222	187,515	10,798	466,530	284,883	128,825	37,014	539,355	156,636	26,556	245,515	206,660	55,341
empty	6,377	35,844	22,389	0	0	99	0	8,112	0	4,857	0	470	0	1,988	0	0	0
train [%]	77.6	81.0	78.3	81.6	80.3	78.9	81.2	80.0	80.1	81.1	81.3	80.1	78.9	79.3	82.8	83.6	81.5
dev [%]	11.4	14.2	10.6	10.4	10.2	10.5	10.7	10.0	10.0	9.6	9.2	10.0	13.5	10.2	8.8	8.7	8.8
test [%]	11.0	4.9	11.2	8.1	9.5	10.6	8.1	10.0	10.0	9.4	9.6	9.9	7.6	10.5	8.4	7.7	9.7

Table 4: CorefUD v1.1 statistics. Last 4 datasets are newly introduced, the rest is presented in previous versions.

System	AVG	ca_ancora	cs_pcedt	cs_pdt	de_parcorfull	de_potsdamcc	en_gum	en_parcorfull	es_ancora	fr_democrat	hu_szegedkoref	lt_lcc	pl_pcc	ru_rucor	hu_korkor	no_bokmaalnaarc	no_nynorsknarc	tr_itcc
CorPipe	**74.90 (1)**	**82.59 (1)**	**79.33 (1)**	**79.20 (1)**	**72.12 (1)**	**71.09 (1)**	**76.57 (1)**	**69.86 (1)**	**83.39 (1)**	**69.82 (1)**	**69.47 (1)**	**75.87 (1)**	**79.54 (1)**	**82.46 (1)**	**68.92 (1)**	**78.74 (1)**	**78.77 (1)**	**55.63 (1)**
Anonymous	70.41 (2)	79.51 (2)	75.88 (2)	76.39 (2)	64.37 (3)	68.24 (5)	72.29 (2)	59.02 (3)	80.52 (2)	66.13 (2)	66.25 (2)	70.09 (2)	77.58 (2)	80.19 (2)	64.65 (3)	75.32 (2)	73.33 (2)	47.22 (2)
Ondfa	69.19 (3)	76.02 (3)	74.82 (3)	74.67 (3)	71.86 (2)	69.37 (3)	71.56 (3)	61.62 (2)	77.18 (3)	60.32 (4)	65.75 (4)	68.52 (3)	76.90 (3)	76.50 (4)	66.38 (2)	72.39 (4)	70.91 (4)	41.52 (4)
McGill	65.43 (4)	71.75 (4)	67.67 (7)	70.88 (4)	41.58 (7)	70.20 (2)	66.72 (4)	47.27 (4)	73.78 (4)	65.17 (3)	65.93 (3)	65.77 (6)	76.14 (4)	77.28 (3)	60.74 (4)	73.73 (3)	72.43 (3)	45.28 (3)
DeepBlueAI	62.29 (5)	67.55 (7)	70.38 (4)	69.93 (5)	48.81 (5)	63.90 (7)	63.58 (6)	43.33 (5)	69.52 (5)	55.69 (6)	63.14 (5)	66.75 (4)	73.11 (5)	74.41 (5)	54.38 (5)	69.86 (6)	68.53 (5)	36.14 (8)
DFKI-Adapt	61.86 (6)	68.21 (6)	68.72 (5)	67.34 (6)	52.52 (4)	69.28 (4)	65.11 (5)	36.87 (7)	69.19 (6)	58.96 (5)	58.56 (6)	66.01 (5)	67.98 (6)	72.48 (6)	51.53 (7)	70.05 (5)	68.21 (6)	40.67 (5)
Morphbase	59.53 (7)	68.23 (5)	64.89 (8)	64.74 (8)	39.96 (9)	64.87 (6)	62.80 (8)	40.81 (6)	69.01 (7)	53.18 (8)	56.41 (7)	64.08 (7)	67.88 (7)	68.53 (8)	52.91 (6)	68.17 (7)	66.35 (7)	39.22 (6)
BASELINE	56.96 (8)	65.26 (8)	67.72 (6)	65.22 (7)	44.11 (6)	57.13 (9)	63.08 (7)	35.19 (8)	66.93 (8)	55.31 (7)	55.32 (8)	63.57 (8)	66.08 (8)	69.03 (7)	40.71 (9)	65.10 (9)	65.78 (8)	22.75 (9)
DFKI-MPrompt	53.76 (9)	55.45 (9)	60.39 (9)	56.13 (9)	40.34 (8)	59.75 (8)	57.83 (9)	34.32 (9)	58.31 (9)	52.96 (9)	48.79 (9)	56.52 (9)	61.15 (9)	61.96 (9)	44.53 (8)	65.12 (8)	62.99 (9)	37.44 (7)

Table 5: This table presents the performances of the participated models in the CRAC 2023 Shared Task. These scores are the average CoNLL F-scores of the all languages. The numbers existing in parentheses indicate the rank of the team for each related language and dataset.

ÚFAL CorPipe at CRAC 2023: Larger Context Improves Multilingual Coreference Resolution

Milan Straka
Charles University, Faculty of Mathematics and Physics
Institute of Formal and Applied Linguistics
Malostranské nám. 25, Prague, Czech Republic
straka@ufal.mff.cuni.cz

Abstract

We present CorPipe, the winning entry to the CRAC 2023 Shared Task on Multilingual Coreference Resolution. Our system is an improved version of our earlier multilingual coreference pipeline, and it surpasses other participants by a large margin of 4.5 percent points. CorPipe first performs mention detection, followed by coreference linking via an antecedent-maximization approach on the retrieved spans. Both tasks are trained jointly on all available corpora using a shared pretrained language model. Our main improvements comprise inputs larger than 512 subwords and changing the mention decoding to support ensembling. The source code is available at https://github.com/ufal/crac2023-corpipe.

1 Introduction

The goal of coreference resolution is to identify and cluster multiple occurrences of entities in the input text. The CRAC 2023 Shared Task on Multilingual Coreference Resolution (Žabokrtský et al., 2023) aims to stimulate research in this area by featuring coreference resolution on 17 corpora in 12 languages from the CorefUD 1.1 dataset (Novák et al., 2022). The current shared task is a reiteration of the previous year's CRAC 2022 Shared Task (Žabokrtský et al., 2022).

CorPipe, our entry to the CRAC 2023 Shared Task, is an improved version of our earlier multilingual coreference pipeline (Straka and Straková, 2022), which was the winner of the last year's shared task. Our system first performs mention detection, followed by the coreference linking via an antecedent-maximization approach on the retrieved spans. However, CorPipe is not a pure pipeline, because we train both tasks jointly using a shared pretrained language model. Performing mention detection first avoids the challenge of end-to-end systems that need to consider an overwhelming number of possible spans, and also permits recognition of single-mention entities. Finally, all our models are multilingual and are trained on all available corpora.

Our contributions are as follows:

- We present a winning entry to the CRAC 2023 Shared Task with state-of-the-art results, surpassing other shared task participants by a large margin of 4.5 percent points.
- We improve our last year's system by (a) increasing the size of the inputs during prediction, while keeping it smaller during training, (b) using larger pretrained language models, (c) proposing a different mention decoding approach, that allows (d) implementing ensembling to further improve the performance.
- We perform a thorough examination of the newly introduced components.
- The source code of our system is available at https://github.com/ufal/crac2023-corpipe.

2 Related Work

While coreference resolution was traditionally carried out by first performing mention detection followed by coreference linking (clustering), recent approaches are often end-to-end (Lee et al., 2017, 2018). Likewise, the baseline of CRAC 2022 and 2023 Shared Tasks (Pražák et al., 2021) as well as the CRAC 2022 second-best solution (Pražák and Konopik, 2022) follow this approach.

The recent work of Bohnet et al. (2023) pushes the end-to-end approach even further, solving both mention detection and coreference linking jointly via a text-to-text paradigm, reaching state-of-the-art results on the CoNLL 2012 dataset (Pradhan et al., 2012). Given that our system uses the same pretrained encoder but a custom decoder designed specifically for coreference resolution instead of a general but pretrained decoder, it would be interesting to perform a direct comparison of these systems.

Proceedings of the CRAC 2023 Shared Task on Multilingual Coreference Resolution, pages 41–51
December 7, 2023

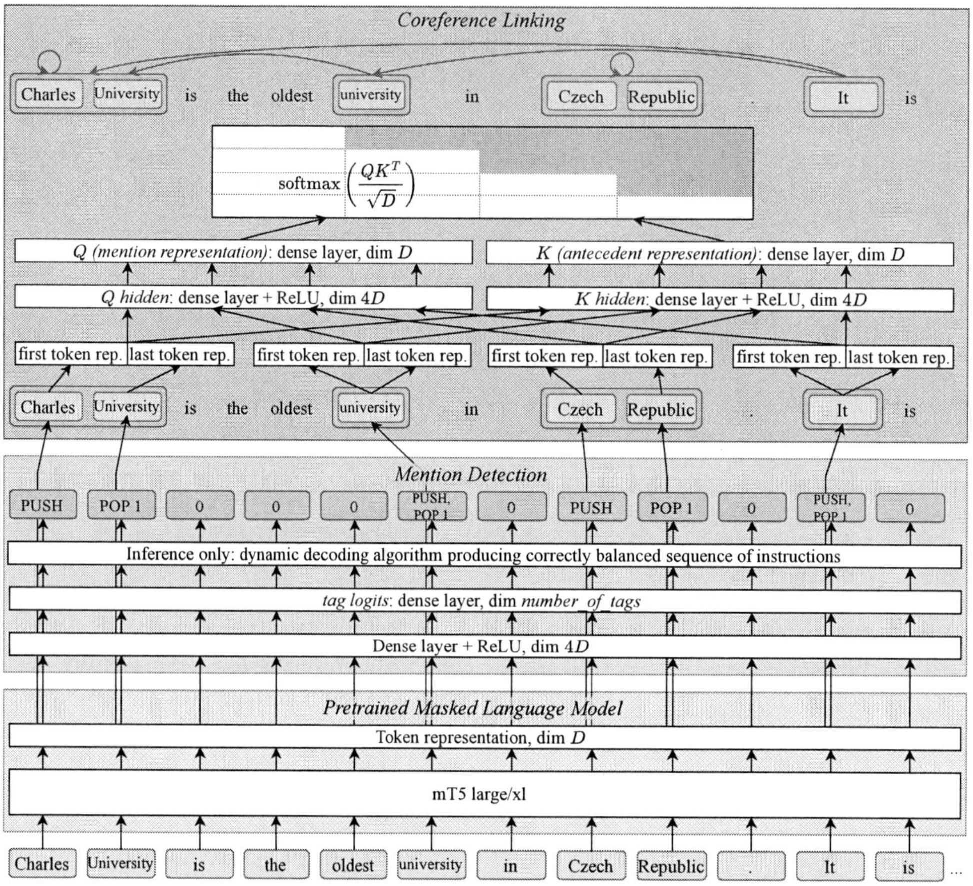

Figure 1: The proposed CorPipe model architecture.

3 CorPipe Architecture

The CorPipe architecture is based heavily on our earlier system (Straka and Straková, 2022), which won the CRAC 2022 Shared Task (Žabokrtský et al., 2022). We describe just the changes we propose; please refer to (Straka and Straková, 2022) for the description of our original system.

In short, our system first obtains a contextualized representation of the input by employing a pretrained model. These representations are then used first to perform mention detection, and then, together with the predicted mentions, to perform coreference linking. The mentions are predicted one sentence at a time, but both previous and following contexts are included up to the specified *context length*. The architecture overview is displayed in Figure 1.

3.1 The mT5 Pretrained Models

In the original architecture, we employed large-sized models XLM-R large (Conneau et al., 2020) and RemBERT (Chung et al., 2021). However, even bigger models consistently deliver better performance in various applications (Kale and Rastogi, 2020; Xue et al., 2021; Rothe et al., 2021; Bohnet et al., 2023). We therefore decided to utilize the largest possible pretrained multilingual model. To our best knowledge, we are aware of a single family of such models, the mT5 (Xue et al., 2021), a multilingual variant of the encoder-decoder pretrained model T5 (Kale and Rastogi, 2020) based on the Transformer architecture (Vaswani et al., 2017).[1]

The mT5 pretrained models have one more considerable advantage – because of relative positional embeddings, they are capable of processing inputs longer than 512 subwords, compared to both XLM-R large and RemBERT. In Section 5.1, we demonstrate that processing longer inputs is advantageous for coreference resolution.

[1]The ByT5 (Xue et al., 2022), a byte version of multilingual T5, is also available, but because it represents words as individual UTF-8 bytes, it processes smaller inputs compared to mT5, which is undesirable for coreference resolution.

3.2 Mention Decoding

In the original architecture, we reduce the representation of embedded and possibly crossing mentions to a sequence classification problem using an extension of BIO encoding. Each input token is assigned a single tag, which is a concatenation of a sequence of stack-manipulating instructions:

- any number of POP(i) instructions, each closing an opened mention from the stack. To support crossing mentions, any mention on the stack (not just the top one) can be closed, identified by its index i from the top of the stack (i.e., POP(1) closes the mention on the top of the stack, POP(2) closes the mention below the top of the stack);
- any number of PUSH instructions, each starting a new mention added to the top of the stack;
- any number of POP(1) instructions, each closing a single-token mention started by a PUSH instruction from the same tag (such single-token mentions could be also represented by a dedicated instruction like UNIT, but we prefer smaller number of instructions).

To produce hopefully valid (well-balanced) sequences of tags, we originally used a linear-chain conditional random fields (CRF; Lafferty et al. 2001). Because of the Markovian property, every tag had to be parametrized also with the size of the stack before the first instruction (we call these tags the *depth-dependent tags*).

The described approach has two drawbacks. First, the predicted sequence of tags might still be unbalanced (which we observed repeatedly in the predictions). Furthermore, it would be more challenging to perform ensembling, because every model would have a different sequence-based partition function.[2]

To alleviate both mentioned issues, we propose to replace the CRF with per-token classification during training and perform a constrained dynamic programming decoding during inference using the Viterbi algorithm.[3] Such approach admits ensembling in a straightforward manner by averaging predicted distributions for each token independently.

Without the CRF, the tags no longer need to be parametrized by the current size of the stack – the depth of the stack can be tracked just during decoding (we consider stack depths of at most 10; Section 5.2 demonstrates that depth 3 is actually sufficient). Such *depth-independent tags* have the advantage of being scarcer,[4] admitting better statistical efficiency, and we utilize them in our primary submission. The comparison of both tag sets as well as the CRF and dynamic programmic decoding is performed in Section 5.2.

3.3 Multilingual Training Data

All our models are trained on all 17 CorefUD 1.1 corpora. Given that their size range from tiny (457 training sentences in `de` and `en parcorfull`) to large (almost 40k training sentences in `cs pdt` and `cs pcedt`), we try to level the individual corpora performances by sub-/over-sampling the datasets. Concretely, we sample each batch example (a sentence with its context) proportionally to *mix ratios*, the corpora-specific weights. We consider the following possibilities:

- *uniform*: we sample uniformly from all corpora, ignoring their sizes;
- *linear*: we sample proportionally to the sizes of individual corpora;
- *square root*: following (van der Goot et al., 2021), we sample proportionally to the square roots of corpora sizes;
- *logarithmic*: similar to (Straka and Straková, 2022), we sample proportionally to the corpora sizes logarithms, which are linearly rescaled so that the largest corpus is ten times more probable than the smallest corpus.

Since different corpora might require particular annotations, we also consider adding a *corpus id* subword (dataset label) to the input to indicate the dataset of origin and the required style of annotations. These *corpus ids*, evaluated already in (Straka and Straková, 2022), are just a different implementation of treebank embeddings proposed in Stymne et al. (2018).

---

[2]When ensembling models, we average the *distributions* the models predict; in other words, unnormalized logits must first be normalized into (log-)probabilities. While this is straightforward for simple classification, CRF models normalize over all possible label sequences. Ensembling several CRF models would therefore require that, during each step of the sequential decoding of token labels, every model computed the *(log-)probabilities* of all sequences with the label in question conditioned on the already decoded labels. Such an algorithm would have the same asymptotic complexity as the usual CRF decoding times the number of models. However, we did not implement it ourselves.

[3]The decoding algorithm differs from CRF decoding in just two aspects: (a) the logits are normalized into log-probabilities for each token separately, (b) the transition matrix only forbids invalid transitions, all valid transitions have the same weight.

[4]There are 54 and 207 unique *depth-independent* and *depth-dependent tags* in the whole training data, respectively.

System	Avg	ca	cs pcedt	cs pdt	de parc	de pots	en gum	en parc	es	fr	hu korko	hu szege	lt	no bookm	no nynor	pl	ru	tr
ÚFAL CorPipe	**74.90** **1**	**82.59** **1**	**79.33** **1**	**79.20** **1**	**72.12** **1**	**71.09** **1**	**76.57** **1**	**69.86** **1**	**83.39** **1**	**69.82** **1**	**68.92** **1**	**69.47** **1**	**75.87** **1**	**78.74** **1**	**78.77** **1**	**79.54** **1**	**82.46** **1**	**55.63** **1**
Anonymous	70.41 2	79.51 2	75.88 2	76.39 2	64.37 3	68.24 5	72.29 2	59.02 3	80.52 2	66.13 2	64.65 3	66.25 2	70.09 2	75.32 2	73.33 2	77.58 2	80.19 2	47.22 2
Ondfa	69.19 3	76.02 3	74.82 3	74.67 3	71.86 2	69.37 3	71.56 3	61.62 2	77.18 3	60.32 4	66.38 2	65.75 4	68.52 3	72.39 4	70.91 4	76.90 3	76.50 4	41.52 4
McGill	65.43 4	71.75 4	67.67 7	70.88 4	41.58 7	70.20 2	66.72 4	47.27 4	73.78 4	65.17 3	60.74 4	65.93 3	65.77 6	73.73 3	72.43 3	76.14 4	77.28 3	45.28 3
DeepBlueAI	62.29 5	67.55 7	70.38 4	69.93 5	48.81 5	63.90 7	63.58 6	43.33 5	69.52 5	55.69 6	54.38 5	63.14 5	66.75 4	69.86 6	68.53 5	73.11 5	74.41 5	36.14 8
DFKI-Adapt	61.86 6	68.21 6	68.72 5	67.34 6	52.52 4	69.28 4	65.11 5	36.87 7	69.19 6	58.96 5	51.53 7	58.56 6	66.01 5	70.05 5	68.21 6	67.98 6	72.48 6	40.67 5
Morfbase	59.53 7	68.23 5	64.89 8	64.74 8	39.96 9	64.87 6	62.80 8	40.81 6	69.01 7	53.18 8	52.91 6	56.41 7	64.08 7	68.17 7	66.35 7	67.88 7	68.53 8	39.22 6
BASELINE†	56.96 8	65.26 8	67.72 6	65.22 7	44.11 6	57.13 9	63.08 7	35.19 8	66.93 8	55.31 7	40.71 9	55.32 8	63.57 8	65.10 9	65.78 8	66.08 8	69.03 7	22.75 9
DFKI-MPrompt	53.76 9	55.45 9	60.39 9	56.13 9	40.34 8	59.75 8	57.83 9	34.32 9	58.31 9	52.96 9	44.53 8	48.79 9	56.52 9	65.12 8	62.99 9	61.15 9	61.96 9	37.44 7

Table 1: Official results of CRAC 2023 Shared Task on the test set (CoNLL score in %). The system † is described in Pražák et al. (2021); the rest in Žabokrtský et al. (2023).

Our primary submission relies on *logarithmic* mix ratios with *corpus ids*. The concrete values of all proposed mix ratios together with their performance comparison are presented in Section 5.5.

3.4 Training

When utilizing the mT5 pretrained models, we train CorPipe models with the Adafactor optimizer (Shazeer and Stern, 2018) using a slanted triangular learning schedule – we first linearly increase the learning rate from 0 to `5e-4` in the first 10% of the training, and then linearly decay it to 0 at the end of the training. The models are trained for 15 epochs, each comprising 8000 batches. For models up to size large, we utilize batch size 8, which is the maximum one fitting on a single A100 GPU with 40GB RAM. The xl-sized models are trained on four 40GB A100, with a maximum possible batch size 12. The training took 10 and 20 hours for the mT5-large and mT5-xl models, respectively.

For the XLM-R and RemBERT ablation experiments, we utilize the lazy variant of the Adam optimizer (Kingma and Ba, 2015) and the learning rates of `2e-5` and `1e-5`, respectively.

All classification heads employ label smoothing (Szegedy et al., 2016) of 0.2.

During training, we use *context length* of 512 subwords and limit the right context length to 50, but we use *context length* of 2560 subwords during inference with the mT5 models.

The competition submissions were selected from a pool of 30 models based on mT5-large and mT5-xl pretrained models with different random seeds and slightly perturbed hyperparameters,[5] by considering for each corpus the best performing checkpoint of every epoch of every trained model. Our primary submission is for each corpus an ensemble of 3 best checkpoints of 3 models.[6]

[5] Learning rate `5e-4`, `6e-4`, `7e-4`; double or quadruple batch size; 8k or 10k batches per epoch.

System	Head-match	Partial-match	Exact-match	+Singletons
ÚFAL CorPipe	**74.90 (1)**	**73.33 (1)**	**71.46 (1)**	**76.82 (1)**
Anonymous	70.41 (2)	69.23 (2)	67.09 (2)	73.20 (2)
Ondfa	69.19 (3)	68.93 (3)	53.01 (8)	68.37 (3)
McGill	65.43 (4)	64.56 (4)	63.13 (3)	68.23 (4)
DeepBlueAI	62.29 (5)	61.32 (5)	59.95 (4)	54.51 (5)
DFKI-Adapt	61.86 (6)	60.83 (6)	59.18 (5)	53.94 (6)
Morfbase	59.53 (7)	58.49 (7)	56.89 (6)	52.07 (7)
BASELINE	56.96 (8)	56.28 (8)	54.75 (7)	49.32 (8)
DFKI-MPrompt	53.76 (9)	51.62 (9)	50.42 (9)	46.83 (9)

Table 2: Official results of CRAC 2023 Shared Task on the test set with various metrics in %.

4 Shared Task Results

The official results of the CRAC 2023 Shared Task are presented in Table 1. Our CorPipe system delivers the best overall score of 74.9%, surpassing the other participants by a large margin of 4.5 percent points, and also achieves the best scores for all individual corpora.

4.1 Results of Additional Metrics

The CRAC 2023 Shared Task primary metric employs *head matching*, where a predicted mention is considered correct if it has the same mention head as the gold mention, and excludes *singletons*. Comparison with other metrics is performed in Table 2. Apart from the head matching, the organizers evaluated also *partial matching* (a predicted mention is correct if it is a subsequence of the gold mention

[6] We implemented ensembling by loading each model to its dedicated A100 GPU, thus parallelizing the execution of the individual models.

Submission	Avg	ca	cs pcedt	cs pdt	de parc	de pots	en gum	en parc	es	fr	hu korko	hu szege	lt	no bookm	no nynor	pl	ru	tr
Original CorPipe 2022	70.3	79.9	76.0	76.8	63.3	**72.6**	72.3	57.6	81.2	65.4	66.2	65.4	68.6	75.4	73.6	79.0	78.4	42.5
Single mT5 large model	+2.6	+2.2	+2.1	+0.8	+6.7	−1.2	+1.6	+4.0	+0.9	+0.1	+1.6	+3.3	**+7.4**	**+3.5**	+2.2	−0.5	+2.4	+7.6
Single mT5 xl model	+2.7	+2.0	+2.0	+1.5	+2.7	−3.0	+2.9	+6.8	+1.6	+2.6	−0.7	**+4.1**	+4.7	+3.3	+3.7	−0.3	+2.6	+10.3
Per-treebank best mT5 model	+3.4	+2.6	+1.7	+1.6	**+13.1**	−4.1	+3.2	+10.3	+1.2	+3.3	−0.2	+2.0	+6.6	+3.0	+4.2	−0.8	+3.8	+7.6
Per-treebank 3-model ensemble	**+4.6**	**+2.7**	**+3.3**	**+2.4**	+8.8	−1.5	**+4.3**	**+12.3**	**+2.2**	**+4.4**	**+2.7**	+4.1	+7.3	+3.3	**+5.2**	**+0.5**	**+4.1**	**+13.1**
Per-treebank 8-model ensemble	*+4.9*	*+3.3*	*+3.3*	*+2.7*	*+7.7*	*−0.8*	*+4.2*	*+13.4*	*+2.3*	*+3.2*	*+3.3*	*+5.4*	*+7.8*	*+4.2*	*+5.4*	*+0.8*	*+4.2*	*+14.0*

Table 3: Official results of ablation experiments on the test set (CoNLL score in %). The 8-model ensemble (in italics) was evaluated during the post-competition phase.

and contains the gold mention head), *exact matching* (a predicted mention is correct if it is exactly equal to the gold mention), and head matching including *singletons* (entities with a single mention).

The ranking of all systems is unchanged in all evaluated metrics, with a single exception – the system *Ondfa* exhibits low exact-matching performance, presumably because it reduces predicted mentions to just their heads.[7]

4.2 Results of Our Additional Submissions

To quantify this year's CorPipe improvements, we present the official results of our additional submissions in Table 3.

We first trained the original CorPipe on this year's data, achieving a 70.3% CoNLL score, which is 0.1 percent points below the second-best submission. Incorporating mT5-large/mT5-xl models, context size of 2560, and constrained decoding with depth-independent tags resulted in an increase of 3.4 percent points. Furthermore, employing a 3-model ensemble provides another 1.2 percent points raise. In the post-competition phase, we also evaluated an 8-model ensemble, which delivered a final modest improvement of 0.3 percent points and reached our best performance of 75.2%.

All these submissions choose the best model checkpoints for every corpus independently. However, for deployment, a single checkpoint is more appropriate – therefore, we also assessed the single best-performing mT5-large checkpoint, resulting in a 72.9% score (0.8 percent points lower than choosing the best mT5-large/mT5-xl checkpoint per corpus). The single best-performing mT5-xl checkpoint achieved very similar performance of 73.0%. We note that these single-checkpoint submissions would comfortably win the shared task too.

[7]Reducing mentions to heads was a strategy for improving partial-matching score in the previous edition of the shared task; with the head-matching score, it can be avoided, which allows also correct evaluation of the exact matching.

5 Ablations on the Development Set

To evaluate the effect of various hyperparameters, we perform further experiments on the development set. Because we observed a significant variance with different random seeds and we also observed divergence in some training runs, we devised the following procedure to obtain credible results: For each configuration, we perform 7 training runs and keep only the 5 ones with the best overall performance. We then want to perform early stopping for every corpus. However, choosing for every corpus a different epoch in every run could lead to maximization bias in case the results oscillate considerably – therefore, for every corpus, we choose the single epoch achieving the highest average 5-run score (i.e., we use this epoch for all 5 runs). Finally, we either average or ensemble the 5 runs for every corpus.

5.1 Pretrained Models and Context Sizes

The effect of increasing context sizes on the mT5-large pretrained model is presented in Table 4.A. The performance improves consistently with increasing context size up to 2560; however, context size 4096 deteriorates the performance slightly. Considering context size 512, decreasing the context size by 128 to 384 decreases the performance by 1.6 percent points, while increasing the context size by 128 to 768 increases it by 1.2 percent points, with performance improving up to 2 percent points for context length 2560.

For the mT5-xl pretrained model, the behavior is virtually analogous, as captured by Table 4.B.

In Table 4.C, we compare the performance of different pretrained models using the context size 512. We include different sizes of the mT5 model (Xue et al., 2021), together with RemBERT (Chung et al., 2021), XLM-R base, and XLM-R large (Conneau et al., 2020).[8]

[8]We do not include other base-sized models like XLM-V (Liang et al., 2023) or mDeBERTaV3 (He et al., 2023), because they lack behind the large-sized models.

Configuration	Avg	ca	cs pcedt	cs pdt	de parc	de pots	en gum	en parc	es	fr	hu korko	hu szege	lt	no bookm	no nynor	pl	ru	tr
A) CONTEXT SIZES FOR THE MT5-LARGE MODEL																		
mT5-large 512	72.8	78.1	78.1	76.9	**70.7**	**75.4**	75.6	**67.4**	80.3	68.6	**70.6**	67.3	77.4	77.8	78.7	75.8	71.1	48.6
mT5-large 256	−5.9	−8.8	−4.0	−5.3	−7.1	−3.2	−5.3	−11.7	−6.0	−4.1	−2.9	−4.5	−8.6	−6.4	−6.4	−4.8	−6.7	−4.6
mT5-large 384	−1.6	−2.9	−1.3	−1.8	−0.6	−0.3	−2.0	−1.6	−2.2	−1.3	−1.4	−1.1	−2.7	−2.4	−2.6	−1.2	−2.0	−1.5
mT5-large 768	+1.2	+2.5	+1.2	+1.5	−0.7	**+0.0**	+0.9	−1.4	+1.5	+1.3	−0.6	+2.1	+0.4	+2.7	+2.2	+0.4	+2.7	+3.3
mT5-large 1024	+1.6	+3.2	+1.8	+1.9	−1.0	**+0.0**	+1.1	−1.4	+2.1	+1.7	−1.1	+2.3	**+0.5**	+3.5	+2.6	+0.7	+3.6	+4.7
mT5-large 1536	+1.9	+3.3	+2.2	+2.1	−1.0	**+0.0**	+1.2	−1.4	+2.4	+1.5	−1.1	+2.4	**+0.5**	**+3.8**	**+3.1**	+1.0	+4.1	+6.8
mT5-large 2048	+2.0	+3.5	+2.2	**+2.1**	−1.0	**+0.0**	**+1.2**	−1.4	+2.5	**+2.0**	−1.1	+2.4	**+0.5**	+3.8	+3.0	+1.2	+4.1	+7.4
mT5-large 2560	**+2.0**	**+3.5**	**+2.2**	+2.1	−1.0	**+0.0**	**+1.2**	−1.4	**+2.5**	+1.7	−1.1	**+2.5**	**+0.5**	+3.7	+3.0	**+1.3**	+4.1	**+8.6**
mT5-large 4096	+1.7	+3.4	+2.1	+2.0	−1.0	**+0.0**	**+1.2**	−1.4	+2.5	+1.5	−1.1	**+2.5**	**+0.5**	+3.7	+2.8	+1.2	**+4.4**	+3.1
B) CONTEXT SIZES FOR THE MT5-XL MODEL																		
mT5-xl 512	73.3	77.5	78.4	77.2	**73.9**	76.1	75.4	72.9	80.1	68.4	**70.3**	67.2	77.2	77.7	78.3	76.1	71.3	47.6
mT5-xl 256	−6.1	−8.6	−3.9	−5.4	−9.2	−3.7	−5.8	−9.6	−5.7	−4.9	−2.8	−4.6	−10.1	−6.1	−6.5	−4.7	−6.7	−4.7
mT5-xl 384	−1.7	−2.6	−1.3	−1.9	−2.4	+0.1	−1.6	−0.4	−2.2	−1.5	−1.6	−1.2	−2.5	−2.2	−2.3	−1.3	−2.5	−0.6
mT5-xl 768	+1.1	+2.2	+1.3	+1.7	−4.4	+0.1	+1.3	+0.9	+1.7	+1.5	−1.3	+1.9	**+1.5**	+2.6	+2.2	+0.5	+2.6	+2.4
mT5-xl 1024	+1.5	+3.2	+1.9	+2.3	−4.4	**+0.1**	+1.5	**+1.0**	+2.3	+2.1	−1.5	+2.1	+1.2	+3.3	+2.9	+0.8	+3.9	+3.2
mT5-xl 1536	+1.8	+3.4	+2.4	+2.6	−4.4	**+0.1**	+1.7	**+1.0**	+2.7	**+2.1**	−1.5	+2.2	+1.2	**+3.8**	+3.5	+1.1	+5.2	+3.5
mT5-xl 2048	+1.8	**+3.5**	+2.6	**+2.6**	−4.4	+0.1	+1.7	**+1.0**	+2.8	+2.1	−1.5	**+2.2**	+1.2	+3.7	**+3.9**	+1.3	**+5.5**	+3.6
mT5-xl 2560	**+1.9**	+3.4	+2.6	+2.6	−4.4	+0.1	+1.7	**+1.0**	+2.8	+2.0	−1.5	+2.2	+1.2	+3.7	+3.6	**+1.4**	+5.3	**+5.7**
mT5-xl 4096	+1.7	+3.5	**+2.6**	+2.5	−4.4	+0.1	**+1.7**	**+1.0**	**+2.8**	+1.8	−1.5	+2.2	+1.2	+3.6	+3.6	+1.4	+5.3	+2.6
C) PRETRAINED LANGUAGE MODELS WITH CONTEXT SIZE 512																		
mT5-large 512	72.8	78.1	78.1	76.9	70.7	75.4	75.6	67.4	80.3	68.6	**70.6**	67.3	77.4	77.8	78.7	75.8	71.1	**48.6**
mT5-small 512	−9.7	−10.2	−11.3	−11.9	−10.6	−11.9	−8.0	−2.8	−9.5	−8.4	−12.7	−8.6	−8.1	−7.0	−9.2	−11.2	−11.6	−12.8
mT5-base 512	−3.9	−4.2	−4.1	−4.5	−3.8	−5.2	−3.8	+1.2	−3.6	−3.3	−8.3	−3.8	−1.6	−3.3	−3.0	−4.3	−4.6	−7.1
XLM-R-base 512	−1.9	−2.8	−3.4	−4.0	−0.5	−3.9	−3.5	+2.4	−2.6	−1.5	−2.8	−1.7	+0.9	−1.8	−2.3	−3.3	−0.8	−2.3
XLM-R-large 512	**+1.1**	**+1.2**	+0.7	**+0.9**	+1.5	+0.8	**+0.8**	+2.7	**+0.9**	**+1.7**	−0.9	**+2.7**	**+1.0**	**+1.2**	**+1.0**	+0.6	+2.1	−0.8
RemBERT 512	+0.2	+0.7	**+1.2**	+0.7	**+3.4**	**+2.5**	+0.1	+4.2	+0.5	+1.0	−3.3	+0.0	−1.1	+0.0	+0.0	**+0.9**	**+2.2**	−10.0
mT5-xl 512	+0.5	−0.6	+0.3	+0.3	+3.2	+0.7	−0.2	**+5.5**	−0.2	−0.2	−0.3	−0.1	−0.2	−0.1	−0.4	+0.3	+0.2	−1.0
D) COMPARISON OF PRETRAINED LANGUAGE MODELS WITH DIFFERENT CONTEXT SIZES																		
mT5-large 512	72.8	78.1	78.1	76.9	70.7	75.4	75.6	67.4	80.3	68.6	**70.6**	67.3	77.4	77.8	78.7	75.8	71.1	48.6
mT5-base 512	−3.9	−4.2	−4.1	−4.5	−3.8	−5.2	−3.8	+1.2	−3.6	−3.3	−8.3	−3.8	−1.6	−3.3	−3.0	−4.3	−4.6	−7.1
XLM-R-base 256	−7.3	−10.0	−6.6	−8.0	−15.1	−5.5	−7.1	−9.8	−7.6	−4.6	−4.4	−4.7	−8.0	−6.3	−8.5	−6.5	−6.9	−5.3
XLM-R-base 384	−4.0	−5.2	−5.0	−5.6	−3.2	−4.1	−5.0	−2.2	−4.9	−2.9	−5.3	−2.8	−2.6	−3.8	−5.2	−3.8	−3.9	−2.5
XLM-R-base 512	−1.9	−2.8	−3.4	−4.0	−0.5	−3.9	−3.5	+2.4	−2.6	−1.5	−2.8	−1.7	+0.9	−1.8	−2.3	−3.3	−0.8	−2.3
XLM-R-base mT5-512	*−3.4*	*−4.9*	*−5.0*	*−5.6*	*−3.4*	*−4.1*	*−4.4*	*−0.6*	*−4.6*	*−2.3*	*−5.0*	*−3.5*	*+0.1*	*−2.9*	*−3.9*	*−3.6*	*−2.3*	*−2.2*
XLM-R-large 256	−3.9	−6.0	−2.8	−3.5	−7.6	−2.1	−3.9	−2.3	−4.1	−2.6	−2.3	−0.7	−7.6	−3.8	−5.0	−2.4	−4.6	−5.3
XLM-R-large 384	−0.7	−1.0	−0.6	−0.5	−1.6	+0.2	+0.0	+1.6	−1.3	+0.1	−2.1	+1.5	−2.5	−1.2	−1.8	+0.0	−0.9	−3.4
XLM-R-large 512	+1.1	+1.2	+0.7	+0.9	+1.5	+0.8	+0.8	+2.7	+0.9	+1.7	−0.9	**+2.7**	**+1.0**	+1.2	+1.0	+0.6	+2.1	−0.8
XLM-R-large mT5-512	*−0.1*	*−0.9*	*−0.6*	*−0.6*	*+0.5*	*+0.4*	*+0.0*	*+2.3*	*−0.9*	*+0.8*	*−2.1*	*+0.8*	*−0.7*	*+0.2*	*−0.4*	*+0.3*	*+0.5*	*−3.0*
RemBERT 256	−4.9	−7.3	−2.4	−3.9	−4.2	+1.0	−4.5	−4.7	−5.4	−3.0	−5.9	−3.5	−9.9	−5.8	−6.3	−3.1	−4.1	−11.3
RemBERT 384	−1.5	−1.9	−0.1	−0.8	+1.1	**+2.8**	−1.5	+0.8	−1.9	−0.3	−5.3	−1.1	−3.6	−2.6	−2.0	−0.1	−0.4	−9.5
RemBERT 512	+0.2	+0.7	+1.2	+0.7	+3.4	+2.5	+0.1	+4.2	+0.5	+1.0	−3.3	+0.0	−1.1	+0.0	+0.0	+0.9	+2.2	−10.0
RemBERT mT5-512	*−0.6*	*−1.0*	*+0.1*	*−0.6*	***+5.4***	*+2.6*	*−0.5*	*+2.3*	*−1.3*	*+0.4*	*−5.4*	*−0.3*	*−1.2*	*−1.0*	*−0.5*	*+0.7*	*+0.5*	*−10.5*
mT5-large 768	+1.2	+2.5	+1.2	+1.5	−0.7	+0.0	+0.9	−1.4	+1.5	+1.3	−0.6	+2.1	+0.4	+2.7	+2.2	+0.4	+2.7	+3.3
mT5-large 2560	+2.0	**+3.5**	+2.2	+2.1	−1.0	+0.0	+1.2	−1.4	+2.5	+1.7	−1.1	+2.5	+0.5	**+3.7**	+3.0	+1.3	+4.1	**+8.6**
mT5-xl 512	+0.5	−0.6	+0.3	+0.3	+3.2	+0.7	−0.2	+5.5	−0.2	−0.2	−0.3	−0.1	−0.2	−0.1	−0.4	+0.3	+0.2	−1.0
mT5-xl 2560	**+2.4**	+2.8	**+2.9**	**+2.9**	−1.2	+0.8	**+1.5**	**+6.5**	**+2.6**	**+1.8**	−1.8	+2.1	+1.0	+3.6	**+3.2**	**+1.7**	**+5.5**	+4.7

Table 4: Ablation experiments evaluated on the development sets (CoNLL score in %). We report the average of best 5 out of 7 runs, using for every corpus the single epoch achieving the highest average 5-run score. The runs in italics use largest context length not exceeding 512 subwords when tokenized with the mT5 tokenizer.

As expected, the increasingly bigger mT5 models improve the performance. Somewhat surprisingly, the XLM-R-base surpasses mT5-base and XLM-R-large and RemBERT surpass mT5-large. However, we discovered that the difference is caused primarily by different tokenization: The mT5 tokenizer produces on average more subwords than the XLM-R and RemBERT tokenizers, which effectively decreases the context size of the mT5 models – but the performance is considerably dependent on the context size.

To expose the issue, Table 4.D compares various pretrained models with different context sizes. Most importantly, we include the performance of the XLM-R and RemBERT models using a context that would be tokenized into 512 subwords by the mT5 tokenizer (presented in italics and denoted by the *mT5-512* context size). In these cases, the performance is quite similar to the performance of the corresponding mT5 model (with the notable exception of RemBERT's performance on Turkish, which is considerably worse). However, the mT5 models support larger context sizes (due to relative positional embeddings); already with context size 768, the mT5 models surpass all models of corresponding size and context size 512, ultimately providing the best results.

Configuration	Label Smoothing	Avg	ca	cs pcedt	cs pdt	de parc	de pots	en gum	en parc	es	fr	hu korko	hu szege	lt	no bookm	no nynor	pl	ru	tr
A) CONSTRAING DECODING WITH VARYING DEPTH AND DEPTH-INDEPENDENT TAGS																			
Depth 10	*0.2*	**74.8**	**81.6**	80.3	**79.0**	69.7	75.4	**76.8**	66.0	82.8	**70.3**	**69.5**	69.8	77.9	81.5	81.7	77.1	75.2	57.2
Depth 3	*0.2*	+0.0	−0.1	**+0.0**	−0.1	+0.0	+0.0	+0.0	+0.0	−0.3	**+0.0**	**+0.0**	+0.0	+0.0	−0.1	**+0.0**	+0.0	+0.0	**+0.0**
Depth 2	*0.2*	−0.2	−0.7	−0.6	−0.9	+0.4	**+0.5**	−0.4	+0.0	−0.9	−0.1	+0.0	+0.0	+0.0	−0.2	−0.1	−0.4	+0.0	**+0.0**
Depth 1	*0.2*	−2.3	−5.9	−5.8	−6.1	−2.3	−1.1	−3.5	−0.4	−7.0	−1.3	−0.7	**+0.1**	+0.2	−2.0	−1.1	−1.9	−0.5	−0.6
Depth 10	*0.0*	−0.1	−0.4	−0.3	−0.2	+1.3	−0.8	−0.6	+0.0	−0.2	−0.2	−1.1	+0.0	+1.0	−0.1	−0.8	−0.1	**+1.1**	−0.6
Depth 3	*0.0*	−0.1	−0.5	−0.3	−0.2	**+1.3**	−0.8	−0.6	+0.0	−0.4	−0.2	−1.1	+0.0	+1.0	−0.1	−0.8	−0.2	**+1.1**	−0.6
Depth 2	*0.0*	−0.3	−1.0	−0.8	−1.0	+1.3	−0.5	−1.0	+0.0	−1.3	−0.2	−1.0	+0.0	+1.0	−0.1	−0.8	−0.6	+1.1	−0.6
Depth 1	*0.0*	−2.5	−6.7	−5.8	−6.3	−1.7	−2.2	−4.8	+0.2	−7.9	−1.6	−1.0	+0.1	**+1.0**	−1.7	−1.5	−2.2	+0.7	−1.1
Depth 10	*0.1*	−0.2	−0.1	−0.2	−0.2	+0.2	+0.2	−0.4	+0.1	**+0.2**	−0.1	−1.4	−0.5	+0.5	**+0.1**	−0.5	**+0.1**	+0.0	−1.6
Depth 3	*0.1*	−0.2	−0.2	−0.2	−0.3	+0.2	+0.2	−0.5	+0.1	+0.0	−0.1	−1.4	−0.5	+0.5	+0.0	−0.5	+0.0	+0.0	−1.6
Depth 2	*0.1*	−0.5	−0.8	−0.7	−1.1	+0.2	+0.4	−0.9	+0.1	−0.8	−0.2	−1.4	−0.5	+0.5	+0.0	−0.7	−0.5	+0.0	−1.6
Depth 1	*0.1*	−2.5	−6.2	−5.9	−6.2	−1.8	−0.9	−4.1	**+0.5**	−7.2	−1.4	−1.7	−0.4	+0.6	−1.8	−1.6	−2.0	−0.5	−2.0
B) COMPARISON OF DIFFERENT DECODING STRATEGIES																			
Constraint decoding, depth 10, depth-independent tags	*0.2*	**74.8**	81.6	80.3	79.0	69.7	75.4	76.8	66.0	**82.8**	70.3	69.5	69.8	77.9	81.5	81.7	77.1	75.2	**57.2**
Greedy, depth-dependent tags	*0.0*	−1.3	−1.1	−1.1	−1.3	−4.6	−0.3	−0.8	−1.5	−1.0	−0.7	−2.4	−1.0	−1.3	−0.8	−0.4	−0.4	−0.2	−3.1
+ constraint decoding	*0.0*	−0.4	−0.6	−0.2	+0.1	−1.6	+0.7	−0.4	−0.1	−0.4	−0.5	−0.5	−0.1	−0.6	−0.5	−0.1	−0.2	−0.3	−1.2
Greedy, depth-dependent tags	*0.1*	−1.3	−1.2	−1.2	−1.4	−3.2	−1.2	−1.0	−7.7	−1.1	−0.1	−1.6	−0.9	+0.5	−0.2	−0.1	−0.1	**+1.4**	−2.6
+ constraint decoding	*0.1*	−0.3	−0.6	−0.4	−0.1	+1.3	−0.1	−0.6	−4.9	−0.5	**+0.2**	**+0.9**	−0.1	**+0.7**	+0.1	**+0.0**	**+0.2**	+1.2	−2.2
Greedy, depth-dependent tags	*0.2*	−1.3	−1.3	−0.9	−1.2	−2.3	−1.0	−0.8	+0.8	−1.1	−0.2	−3.1	−1.1	−2.0	−1.3	−0.6	−0.7	−0.1	−5.4
+ constraint decoding	*0.2*	−0.3	−1.0	−0.3	+0.0	**+2.5**	−0.6	−0.4	**+3.3**	−0.4	+0.0	−0.9	−0.4	−0.3	−0.9	−0.3	−0.5	+0.0	−4.8
Conditional random fields	*0.0*	−0.2	−0.4	−0.3	−0.1	+1.7	−0.7	+0.0	+1.5	−0.5	−0.6	−0.3	+0.3	+0.4	−0.9	−0.4	−0.4	−0.3	−2.2
+ constraint decoding	*0.0*	−0.1	−0.3	−0.3	+0.0	+1.7	−0.6	+0.0	+1.8	−0.3	−0.6	−0.2	**+0.3**	+0.5	−1.0	−0.5	−0.4	−0.3	−2.2
Conditional random fields	*0.1*	−0.2	−0.4	**+0.1**	+0.3	+0.3	−1.1	+0.2	+1.1	−0.1	−0.3	−0.3	−0.2	−0.3	−0.2	−0.1	+0.0	+0.6	−3.6
+ constraint decoding	*0.1*	−0.2	−0.3	+0.1	**+0.4**	+0.5	−1.2	**+0.2**	+0.6	−0.1	−0.2	−0.3	−0.2	−0.2	−0.1	−0.1	−0.1	+0.5	−3.6
Conditional random fields	*0.2*	−0.3	+0.2	−0.3	+0.0	−1.2	+1.1	+0.1	+0.1	−0.2	+0.0	+0.0	+0.0	−1.5	+0.2	+0.0	+0.0	+0.9	−3.9
+ constraint decoding	*0.2*	−0.2	**+0.2**	−0.3	+0.1	−1.4	**+1.2**	+0.1	+0.4	−0.1	+0.1	+0.2	+0.0	−1.5	**+0.2**	−0.1	+0.0	+0.8	−3.9

Table 5: Ablation experiments evaluated on the development sets (CoNLL score in %) using the mT5-large model with context size 2560. We report the average of best 5 out of 7 runs, using for every corpus the single epoch achieving the highest average 5-run score.

5.2 Mention Decoding Algorithms

The effects of the mention decoding algorithm and label smoothing are elaborated in Table 5. First, label smoothing has very little effect on the results.

When predicting mentions via depth-independent tags, the maximum possible number of opened multi-word mentions (*depth*) must be specified. The effect of using depths 1, 2, 3, and 10 is presented in Table 5.A. While the maximum depth in the training data is 12, the performance of using depth 10 and 3 is virtually unchanged; only depth 2 and depth 1 deteriorate performance. If the speed of the decoding is an issue, using depth 3 provides the fastest decoder without decreasing performance.

The difference between using depth-independent and depth-dependent tags during constrained decoding is quantified in Table 5.B – depth-independent tags provide a minor improvement of 0.3 percent points. When greedy decoding is used instead of constrained decoding, the performance drops by one percent point.

Using conditional random fields for mention decoding provides marginally worse performance compared to using constrained decoding with depth-independent tags. Furthermore, explicitly disallowing invalid transitions (by assigning them transition weight $-\infty$ in the transition weight matrix manually) has virtually no effect, demonstrating that the CRF decoder has learned the transition weights successfully.

5.3 The Effect Of Multilingual Data

In Table 6, we analyze the effect of using various combinations of corpora during training.

Compared to using all corpora for single-model training, relying solely on the training data of a given corpus deteriorates the performance dramatically by 3.7 percent points on average. The decrease is smallest for the largest corpora (Czech and Polish ones).

Concatenating all corpora of a given language (and both ParCorFull corpora that are translations of each other; we utilized uniform mix ratios) generally improves the performance compared to using the individual corpora, but does not reach the performance of using all corpora together.

5.4 Zero-shot Multilingual Evaluation

When training without the corpus ids, the model is able to perform prediction on unknown languages. Leveraging this observation, we perform zero-shot

Configuration	Avg	ca	cs pcedt	cs pdt	de parc	de pots	en gum	en parc	es	fr	hu korko	hu szege	lt	no bookm	no nynor	pl	ru	tr
Single Multilingual Model	**74.8**	**81.6**	**80.3**	**79.0**	**69.7**	**75.4**	**76.8**	**66.0**	**82.8**	**70.3**	**69.5**	**69.8**	**77.9**	**81.5**	**81.7**	**77.1**	**75.2**	**57.2**
Per-Corpus Models	−3.7	−1.4	−0.5	−0.4	−7.7	−3.3	−1.6	−7.6	−1.5	−2.0	−9.1	−1.0	−3.0	−2.3	−2.9	−1.0	−2.0	−15.8
Joint Czech Model			−0.1	−0.3														
Joint German Model					−4.8	−3.9												
Joint English Model							−1.9	−4.5										
Joint Parcorfull Model					−4.4			−2.5										
Joint Hungarian Model											−5.9	−1.1						
Joint Norwegian Model														−1.3	−1.8			
Zero-Shot Multilingual Models	−13.2	−4.8	−24.2	−16.0	−13.7	−10.6	−14.4	−13.8	−1.9	−5.4	−15.1	−15.0	−23.4	−14.3	−18.0	−17.5	−15.5	−0.8

Table 6: Ablation experiments evaluated on the development sets (CoNLL score in %) using the mT5-large model with context size 2560. We report the average of best 5 out of 7 runs, using for every corpus the single epoch achieving the highest average 5-run score.

Configuration	Avg	ca	cs pcedt	cs pdt	de parc	de pots	en gum	en parc	es	fr	hu korko	hu szege	lt	no bookm	no nynor	pl	ru	tr
MIX RATIO WEIGHTS OF INDIVIDUAL CORPORA IN PERCENTS																		
Logarithmic		*8.1*	*10.0*	*9.4*	*1.0*	*3.2*	*6.6*	*1.0*	*8.3*	*7.4*	*2.6*	*5.8*	*3.4*	*7.2*	*6.9*	*8.6*	*6.2*	*4.2*
Uniform		*5.9*	*5.9*	*5.9*	*5.9*	*5.9*	*5.9*	*5.9*	*5.9*	*5.9*	*5.9*	*5.9*	*5.9*	*5.9*	*5.9*	*5.9*	*5.9*	*5.9*
Square Root		*8.4*	*14.0*	*11.7*	*1.4*	*2.4*	*5.6*	*1.4*	*8.8*	*6.9*	*2.0*	*4.6*	*2.5*	*6.5*	*6.0*	*9.5*	*5.1*	*3.1*
Linear		*8.7*	*24.4*	*17.0*	*0.2*	*0.7*	*3.9*	*0.2*	*9.6*	*5.9*	*0.5*	*2.6*	*0.8*	*5.3*	*4.5*	*11.3*	*3.2*	*1.2*
A) AVERAGE OF 5 RUNS USING FOR EVERY CORPUS THE SINGLE EPOCH ACHIEVING THE HIGHEST AVERAGE 5-RUN SCORE																		
Logarithmic	74.8	81.6	80.3	79.0	69.7	75.4	**76.8**	66.0	82.8	70.3	69.5	**69.7**	77.9	81.5	81.7	77.1	75.2	**57.2**
w/o corpus id	−0.2	**+0.2**	−0.1	+0.1	−0.4	+0.1	−0.3	−0.2	+0.0	+0.0	−0.2	−0.3	+0.5	**+0.2**	−0.4	**+0.2**	+0.2	−2.4
Uniform	−0.3	−0.1	−1.2	−0.9	+1.7	+0.0	−0.8	−4.2	−0.3	+0.1	**+0.2**	−0.4	**+1.0**	+0.0	−0.1	+0.0	−0.2	−0.1
w/o corpus id	−0.4	−0.4	−0.7	−0.6	+2.3	+0.3	−0.8	+1.5	−0.1	−0.4	−1.3	−0.5	−0.7	−0.4	−1.3	−0.5	−0.2	−3.0
Square Root	+0.0	+0.2	+0.5	+0.4	−0.2	**+0.9**	−0.6	−2.1	−0.1	+0.1	−0.7	−0.1	+0.8	+0.1	−0.2	+0.2	+0.9	−0.7
w/o corpus id	+0.2	+0.1	+0.4	+0.3	**+2.7**	−0.9	−0.3	+1.1	+0.1	+0.0	−0.4	−0.2	+0.1	+0.1	−0.1	+0.1	+0.5	−0.7
Linear	**+0.4**	+0.1	**+0.8**	**+0.7**	+0.6	−0.1	−0.2	**+4.8**	**+0.3**	**+0.4**	−0.9	−0.4	+0.6	−0.3	**+0.1**	+0.2	**+1.1**	−0.3
w/o corpus id	+0.0	+0.0	+0.7	+0.6	−2.0	−1.4	−0.8	+4.0	+0.3	−0.1	−0.4	−0.9	+0.4	+0.1	−0.1	+0.2	+0.7	−0.8
B) AVERAGE OF 5 RUNS USING FOR EVERY RUN THE SINGLE EPOCH ACHIEVING THE HIGHEST SCORE ACROSS ALL CORPORA																		
Logarithmic	74.8	81.7	79.9	78.6	71.5	**76.2**	**76.6**	67.9	82.8	70.4	68.3	69.4	78.0	81.4	81.5	76.9	74.6	55.5
w/o corpus id	−0.2	+0.0	+0.1	+0.2	−1.9	−0.3	−0.3	−0.9	−0.2	−0.4	+0.0	−0.2	−0.2	+0.1	−0.2	+0.3	+1.0	−0.3
Uniform	−0.6	−0.4	−1.1	−0.9	+0.1	−1.0	−0.8	−6.7	−0.4	−0.2	**+1.0**	**+0.1**	−0.2	−0.1	+0.2	−0.1	+0.5	+0.0
w/o corpus id	−0.6	−0.7	−0.6	−0.5	+1.0	−1.6	−0.5	−0.6	−0.1	−0.6	+0.3	−0.5	−0.9	−0.1	−1.3	−0.5	+0.8	−3.0
Square Root	−0.2	−0.1	+0.8	+0.7	−2.5	−0.2	−0.1	−4.2	−0.1	+0.0	+0.9	−0.4	+0.2	+0.3	+0.0	**+0.4**	+1.5	+0.4
w/o corpus id	+0.1	−0.2	+0.6	+0.6	**+1.3**	−2.1	−0.2	−0.7	+0.2	**+0.1**	+0.0	−0.4	−0.1	+0.2	+0.1	+0.1	+1.2	**+1.1**
Linear	**+0.3**	**+0.2**	**+1.1**	**+1.1**	−0.7	−1.9	−0.2	**+3.8**	**+0.5**	−0.1	−0.7	−0.1	+0.3	−0.4	**+0.3**	+0.1	**+1.6**	+0.0
w/o corpus id	+0.1	+0.0	+1.0	+1.0	−2.1	−2.5	−0.2	+1.3	+0.2	−0.1	+0.4	−0.5	**+0.5**	**+0.4**	+0.3	+0.4	+1.0	+0.8

Table 7: Ablation experiments evaluated on the development sets (CoNLL score in %) using the mT5-large model with context size 2560. We report the average of best 5 out of 7 runs.

evaluation by training multilingual models on corpora from all but one language and then evaluating the performance on the omitted-language corpora. The results are displayed on the last line of Table 6.

Overall, the results are significantly worse by 13.2 percent points. However, such performance is most likely better than the performance of the baseline system of Pražák et al. (2021), which has 17.9 less percent points on the test set than CorPipe.

Turkish demonstrates the smallest decrease in the zero-shot evaluation, even when it uses an alphabet with several unique characters. On the other hand, the small decrease in the performance of Catalan, Spanish, and French can be explained by similarities among these languages.

5.5 Mix Ratios of the Multilingual Data

Next, we compare the effect of various mix ratios during all-corpora training.

We consider *logarithmic*, *uniform*, *square root*, and *linear* mix ratios described in Section 3.3. First, their values normalized to percentages are presented in the first part of Table 7.

We then evaluate the effect of using a specific mix ratio and either utilizing or omitting the corpus ids during training in Table 7.A. In accordance with findings in Straka and Straková (2022), the corpus ids have no deterministic effect, and the mix ratios influence the system performance surprisingly little (with *uniform* being the worst, *logarithmic* and *square root* very similar and better, and *linear* the best). When considering the largest corpora (especially Czech, Polish, and Spanish), their performance improves with increasing mix ratios, presumably because of underfitting with small mix ratios; however, the effect on other corpora is mixed.

The evaluation methodology allows each corpus to use a checkpoint from a different epoch of the

Configuration	Avg	ca	cs pcedt	cs pdt	de parc	de pots	en gum	en parc	es	fr	hu korko	hu szege	lt	no bookm	no nynor	pl	ru	tr
A) ENSEMBLES FOR THE MT5-LARGE MODEL FOR VARIOUS CONTEXT SIZES																		
Average of 5 runs, 512	72.8	78.1	78.1	76.9	70.7	75.4	75.6	**67.4**	80.3	68.6	70.6	67.3	77.4	77.8	78.7	75.8	71.1	48.6
Ensemble of 5 runs, 512	+1.0	+0.8	+0.8	+0.7	**+3.1**	**+1.3**	+0.5	–0.4	+0.8	+0.6	**+1.2**	+0.7	+1.6	+0.9	+0.9	+1.0	+1.5	+0.8
Average of 5 runs, 768	+1.2	+2.5	+1.2	+1.5	–0.7	+0.0	+0.9	–1.4	+1.5	+1.3	–0.6	+2.1	+0.4	+2.7	+2.2	+0.4	+2.7	+3.3
Average of 5 runs, 2560	+2.0	+3.5	+2.2	+2.1	–1.0	+0.0	+1.2	–1.4	+2.5	+1.7	–1.1	+2.5	+0.5	+3.7	+3.0	+1.3	+4.1	+8.6
Ensemble of 5 runs, 2560	**+3.3**	**+4.3**	**+3.0**	**+3.0**	+2.3	**+1.3**	**+1.3**	–0.8	**+3.6**	**+2.5**	+1.1	**+3.5**	**+1.8**	**+4.6**	**+3.5**	**+2.3**	**+6.3**	**+11.5**
B) ENSEMBLES FOR THE MT5-XL MODEL FOR VARIOUS CONTEXT SIZES																		
Average of 5 runs, 512	73.3	77.5	78.4	77.2	73.9	76.1	75.4	72.9	80.1	68.4	70.3	67.2	77.2	77.7	78.3	76.1	71.3	47.6
Ensemble of 5 runs, 512	+0.8	+1.1	+0.9	+0.8	–2.3	**+0.2**	+0.8	**+1.9**	+1.1	+1.1	+0.9	+1.8	+1.6	+1.1	+0.8	+1.0	+1.3	+0.3
Average of 5 runs, 768	+1.1	+2.2	+1.3	+1.7	–4.4	+0.1	+1.3	+0.9	+1.7	+1.5	–1.3	+1.9	+1.5	+2.6	+2.2	+0.5	+2.6	+2.4
Average of 5 runs, 2560	+1.9	+3.4	+2.6	+2.6	–4.4	+0.1	+1.7	+1.0	+2.8	+2.0	–1.5	+2.2	+1.2	+3.7	+3.6	+1.4	+5.3	+5.7
Ensemble of 5 runs, 2560	**+3.5**	**+4.9**	**+3.6**	**+3.7**	**+2.4**	**+0.2**	**+2.3**	+1.1	**+3.6**	**+3.3**	**+1.3**	**+4.0**	**+3.0**	**+4.1**	**+5.0**	**+2.5**	**+7.1**	**+7.6**

Table 8: Ablation experiments evaluated on the development sets (CoNLL score in %). We report the average/ensemble of best 5 out of 7 runs, using for every corpus the single epoch achieving the highest average score.

training. Therefore, it could be possible that different mixing ratios influence the best epochs of individual corpora and that with some mixing ratios, the best epochs are more homogeneous. On that account, Table 7.B performs the evaluation differently – for each of the 5 runs, we choose the epoch with the best overall performance on all corpora, and employ the checkpoint from this epoch for all corpora; different runs can utilize different epochs. Nevertheless, the results are very much similar.

5.6 Ensembling

The effect of ensembling the 5 runs (instead of averaging them) is captured in Table 8. For the context size 512, the ensemble delivers an additional 1 percent point with the mT5-large pretrained model and 0.8 percent points with the mT5-xl model. For the context size 2560, the improvement is even slightly larger, 1.3 and 1.6 percent points for the mT5-large and mT5-xl models, respectively.

6 Conclusions

We presented the winning entry to the CRAC 2023 Shared Task on Multilingual Coreference Resolution (Žabokrtský et al., 2023). The system is an improved version of our earlier multilingual coreference pipeline CorPipe (Straka and Straková, 2022), and it surpasses other participants by a large margin of 4.5 percent points. When ensembling is not desired, we also offer a single multilingual checkpoint for all 17 corpora surpassing other submissions by 2.6 percent points. The source code is available at `https://github.com/ufal/crac2023-corpipe`.

Acknowledgements

This work has been supported by the Grant Agency of the Czech Republic, project EXPRO LUSyD (GX20-16819X), and has been using data provided by the LINDAT/CLARIAH-CZ Research Infrastructure (`https://lindat.cz`) of the Ministry of Education, Youth and Sports of the Czech Republic (Project No. LM2023062).

Limitations

The presented system has demonstrated its performance only on a limited set of 12 languages, and heavily depends on a large pretrained model, transitively receiving its limitations and biases.

Furthermore, the practical applicability on plain text inputs depends also on empty node prediction, whose performance has not yet been evaluated.

Training with the mT5-large pretrained model requires a 40GB GPU, which we consider affordable; however, training with the mT5-xl pretrained model needs nearly four times as much GPU memory.

References

Bernd Bohnet, Chris Alberti, and Michael Collins. 2023. Coreference resolution through a seq2seq transition-based system. *Transactions of the Association for Computational Linguistics*, 11:212–226.

Hyung Won Chung, Thibault Fevry, Henry Tsai, Melvin Johnson, and Sebastian Ruder. 2021. Rethinking Embedding Coupling in Pre-trained Language Models. In *International Conference on Learning Representations*.

Alexis Conneau, Kartikay Khandelwal, Naman Goyal, Vishrav Chaudhary, Guillaume Wenzek, Francisco Guzmán, Edouard Grave, Myle Ott, Luke Zettlemoyer, and Veselin Stoyanov. 2020. Unsupervised cross-lingual representation learning at scale. In *Proceedings of the 58th Annual Meeting of the Association for Computational Linguistics*, pages 8440–

8451, Online. Association for Computational Linguistics.

Pengcheng He, Jianfeng Gao, and Weizhu Chen. 2023. DeBERTav3: Improving deBERTa using ELECTRA-style pre-training with gradient-disentangled embedding sharing. In *The Eleventh International Conference on Learning Representations*.

Mihir Kale and Abhinav Rastogi. 2020. Text-to-text pre-training for data-to-text tasks. In *Proceedings of the 13th International Conference on Natural Language Generation*, pages 97–102, Dublin, Ireland. Association for Computational Linguistics.

Diederik P. Kingma and Jimmy Ba. 2015. Adam: A method for stochastic optimization. In *3rd International Conference on Learning Representations, ICLR 2015, San Diego, CA, USA, May 7-9, 2015, Conference Track Proceedings*.

John D. Lafferty, Andrew McCallum, and Fernando C. N. Pereira. 2001. Conditional Random Fields: Probabilistic Models for Segmenting and Labeling Sequence Data. In *Proceedings of the Eighteenth International Conference on Machine Learning*, ICML '01, page 282–289, San Francisco, CA, USA. Morgan Kaufmann Publishers Inc.

Kenton Lee, Luheng He, Mike Lewis, and Luke Zettlemoyer. 2017. End-to-end neural coreference resolution. In *Proceedings of the 2017 Conference on Empirical Methods in Natural Language Processing*, pages 188–197, Copenhagen, Denmark. Association for Computational Linguistics.

Kenton Lee, Luheng He, and Luke Zettlemoyer. 2018. Higher-order coreference resolution with coarse-to-fine inference. In *Proceedings of the 2018 Conference of the North American Chapter of the Association for Computational Linguistics: Human Language Technologies, Volume 2 (Short Papers)*, pages 687–692, New Orleans, Louisiana. Association for Computational Linguistics.

Davis Liang, Hila Gonen, Yuning Mao, Rui Hou, Naman Goyal, Marjan Ghazvininejad, Luke Zettlemoyer, and Madian Khabsa. 2023. XLM-V: Overcoming the Vocabulary Bottleneck in Multilingual Masked Language Models. *arXiv e-prints*, page arXiv:2301.10472.

Michal Novák, Martin Popel, Zdeněk Žabokrtský, Daniel Zeman, Anna Nedoluzhko, Kutay Acar, Peter Bourgonje, Silvie Cinková, Gülşen Cebiroğlu Eryiğit, Jan Hajič, Christian Hardmeier, Dag Haug, Tollef Jørgensen, Andre Kåsen, Pauline Krielke, Frédéric Landragin, Ekaterina Lapshinova-Koltunski, Petter Mæhlum, M.Antònia Martí, Marie Mikulová, Anders Nøklestad, Maciej Ogrodniczuk, Lilja Øvrelid, Tuğba Pamay Arslan, Marta Recasens, Per Erik Solberg, Manfred Stede, Milan Straka, Svetlana Toldova, Noémi Vadász, Erik Velldal, Veronika Vincze, Amir Zeldes, and Voldemaras Žitkus. 2022. Coreference in Universal Dependencies 1.1 (CorefUD 1.1). LINDAT/CLARIAH-CZ digital library at the Institute of Formal and Applied Linguistics (ÚFAL), Faculty of Mathematics and Physics, Charles University.

Sameer Pradhan, Alessandro Moschitti, Nianwen Xue, Olga Uryupina, and Yuchen Zhang. 2012. CoNLL-2012 shared task: Modeling multilingual unrestricted coreference in OntoNotes. In *Joint Conference on EMNLP and CoNLL - Shared Task*, pages 1–40, Jeju Island, Korea. Association for Computational Linguistics.

Ondřej Pražák and Miloslav Konopik. 2022. End-to-end multilingual coreference resolution with mention head prediction. In *Proceedings of the CRAC 2022 Shared Task on Multilingual Coreference Resolution*, pages 23–27, Gyeongju, Republic of Korea. Association for Computational Linguistics.

Ondřej Pražák, Miloslav Konopík, and Jakub Sido. 2021. Multilingual coreference resolution with harmonized annotations. In *Proceedings of the International Conference on Recent Advances in Natural Language Processing (RANLP 2021)*, pages 1119–1123, Held Online. INCOMA Ltd.

Sascha Rothe, Jonathan Mallinson, Eric Malmi, Sebastian Krause, and Aliaksei Severyn. 2021. A simple recipe for multilingual grammatical error correction. In *Proceedings of the 59th Annual Meeting of the Association for Computational Linguistics and the 11th International Joint Conference on Natural Language Processing (Volume 2: Short Papers)*, pages 702–707, Online. Association for Computational Linguistics.

Noam Shazeer and Mitchell Stern. 2018. Adafactor: Adaptive Learning Rates with Sublinear Memory Cost. In *Proceedings of the 35th International Conference on Machine Learning, ICML 2018, Stockholmsmässan, Stockholm, Sweden, July 10-15, 2018*, volume 80 of *Proceedings of Machine Learning Research*, pages 4603–4611. PMLR.

Milan Straka and Jana Straková. 2022. ÚFAL CorPipe at CRAC 2022: Effectivity of multilingual models for coreference resolution. In *Proceedings of the CRAC 2022 Shared Task on Multilingual Coreference Resolution*, pages 28–37, Gyeongju, Republic of Korea. Association for Computational Linguistics.

Sara Stymne, Miryam de Lhoneux, Aaron Smith, and Joakim Nivre. 2018. Parser training with heterogeneous treebanks. In *Proceedings of the 56th Annual Meeting of the Association for Computational Linguistics (Volume 2: Short Papers)*, pages 619–625, Melbourne, Australia. Association for Computational Linguistics.

Christian Szegedy, Vincent Vanhoucke, Sergey Ioffe, Jon Shlens, and Zbigniew Wojna. 2016. Rethinking the Inception Architecture for Computer Vision. In *2016 IEEE Conference on Computer Vision and Pattern Recognition (CVPR)*, pages 2818–2826.

Rob van der Goot, Ahmet Üstün, Alan Ramponi, Ibrahim Sharaf, and Barbara Plank. 2021. Massive choice, ample tasks (MaChAmp): A toolkit for multi-task learning in NLP. In *Proceedings of the 16th Conference of the European Chapter of the Association for Computational Linguistics: System Demonstrations*, pages 176–197, Online. Association for Computational Linguistics.

Ashish Vaswani, Noam Shazeer, Niki Parmar, Jakob Uszkoreit, Llion Jones, Aidan N Gomez, Ł ukasz Kaiser, and Illia Polosukhin. 2017. Attention is All you Need. In *Advances in Neural Information Processing Systems*, volume 30. Curran Associates, Inc.

Linting Xue, Aditya Barua, Noah Constant, Rami Al-Rfou, Sharan Narang, Mihir Kale, Adam Roberts, and Colin Raffel. 2022. ByT5: Towards a token-free future with pre-trained byte-to-byte models. *Transactions of the Association for Computational Linguistics*, 10:291–306.

Linting Xue, Noah Constant, Adam Roberts, Mihir Kale, Rami Al-Rfou, Aditya Siddhant, Aditya Barua, and Colin Raffel. 2021. mT5: A massively multilingual pre-trained text-to-text transformer. In *Proceedings of the 2021 Conference of the North American Chapter of the Association for Computational Linguistics: Human Language Technologies*, pages 483–498, Online. Association for Computational Linguistics.

Zdeněk Žabokrtský, Miloslav Konopík, Anna Nedoluzhko, Michal Novák, Maciej Ogrodniczuk, Martin Popel, Ondřej Pražák, Jakub Sido, and Daniel Zeman. 2023. Findings of the Second Shared Task on Multilingual Coreference Resolution. In *Proceedings of the CRAC 2023 Shared Task on Multilingual Coreference Resolution*, pages 1–18, Singapore. Association for Computational Linguistics.

Zdeněk Žabokrtský, Miloslav Konopík, Anna Nedoluzhko, Michal Novák, Maciej Ogrodniczuk, Martin Popel, Ondřej Pražák, Jakub Sido, Daniel Zeman, and Yilun Zhu. 2022. Findings of the shared task on multilingual coreference resolution. In *Proceedings of the CRAC 2022 Shared Task on Multilingual Coreference Resolution*, pages 1–17, Gyeongju, Republic of Korea. Association for Computational Linguistics.

McGill at CRAC 2023: Multilingual Generalization of Entity-Ranking Coreference Resolution Models

Ian Porada and **Jackie Chi Kit Cheung**

Mila, McGill University
{ian.porada@mail, jcheung@cs}.mcgill.ca

Abstract

Our submission to the CRAC 2023 shared task, described herein, is an adapted entity-ranking model jointly trained on all 17 datasets spanning 12 languages. Our model outperforms the shared task baselines by a difference in F1 score of +8.47, achieving an ultimate F1 score of 65.43 and fourth place in the shared task. We explore design decisions related to data preprocessing, the pretrained encoder, and data mixing.

1 Introduction

The goal of the CRAC 2023 shared task (Žabokrtský et al., 2023) is to evaluate coreference resolution models on the CorefUD 1.1 collection of datasets (Novák et al., 2022). In this paper, we describe our submission to the task, which is an adaptation of the entity-ranking model described in Toshniwal et al. (2020) with some exploration of the design decisions needed to apply this model to multiple datasets spanning multiple languages. Our final submission achieves fourth place out of nine submissions based on head-match F1 score, and third place based on exact-match F1 score.

The CRAC 2023 shared task is specifically based on the public portion of CorefUD 1.1, which includes 17 datasets spanning 12 languages: Catalan, Czech, English, French, German, Hungarian, Lithuanian, Norwegian, Polish, Russian, Spanish, and Turkish. For the final evaluation, gold and predicted mentions are considered matching if they have overlapping head words, referred to as *head-match score*, and the CoNLL F1 head-match score is then macro-averaged over all 17 datasets.

For our submission, we adapt the model described in Toshniwal et al. (2020), which is based on the entity-ranking model originally proposed by Xia et al. (2020). We explore design decisions necessary to apply this English-based model to multilingual coreference resolution: data preprocessing steps, the pretrained language model encoder, and methods of joint training. Our best configuration outperforms the shared task baselines by a difference in head-match F1 score of +8.47, achieving an ultimate score of 65.43.

2 Related Work

Shared tasks have been instrumental in the development and evaluation of coreference resolution systems. Previous examples include CoNLL 2011 (Pradhan et al., 2011), CoNLL 2012 (Pradhan et al., 2012), and GAP (Webster et al., 2018, 2019). The CRAC 2023 shared task builds off the previous iteration, CRAC 2022 (Žabokrtský et al., 2022), with some modification of the datasets and evaluation procedure.

Entity-ranking models (Lee et al., 2017) of coreference resolution function by ranking a set of candidate entities to which each mention might refer. Xia et al. (2020) proposed a competitive neural entity-ranking model that processes mentions incrementally left-to-right. We analyze this method as implemented by Toshniwal et al. (2020). In contrast to existing work, we explore the potential of this model for multilingual generalization.

The best model of the previous CRAC 2022 shared task was that of Straka and Straková (2022), which consists of two stages: mention detection and coreference linking. The authors found that jointly training on multiple datasets led to better performance on the shared task than training several models, one per each individual dataset. The same finding was found in other submissions as well (Pražák and Konopík, 2022).

Existing analyses have considered the generalization of entity-ranking models across datasets, including when jointly trained on multiple datasets (Toshniwal et al., 2021; Xia and Van Durme, 2021; Porada et al., 2023). Although such work has focused on English-language coreference and not evaluated generalization to a multilingual collection of datasets. It is not clear, a priori, how well

Proceedings of the CRAC 2023 Shared Task on Multilingual Coreference Resolution, pages 52–57
December 7, 2023

the constraints of an entity ranking model will generalize to phenomena not present in English coreference datasets such as zero anaphora.

3 Model

We evaluate the entity-ranking model implemented by Toshniwal et al. (2020). In this section, we first overview the model configuration and then outline the design decisions that we explore related to preprocessing, the pretrained encoder, and joint training. The high-level idea of the model is to first use a mention scorer to produce a set of mention candidates, then process the mentions left-to-right to determine if they refer to either a new or existing entity.

Configuration We start with the implementation and hyperparameters of Toshniwal et al. (2021). The model calculates coreference clusters for a document in the following way: first, embeddings are calculated for all spans of ≤ 20 subword tokens using a pretrained encoder. Each span embedding is scored using the mention scoring head described in Joshi et al. (2019), which is based on that originally proposed by Lee et al. (2017). This scoring head is trained with binary cross entropy loss to assign a positive score to annotated mentions and a negative score to all other spans. The top $0.4 \times \ell$ spans are considered as mention candidates and kept for the next step, where ℓ is the length of the document in terms of subword tokens. This set of mention candidates is further filtered by removing all spans with a negative score.

Then, the set of entities is initialized as $E = \{\}$ and the mention candidates are processed in a left-to-right order. When processed, each candidate m is scored against all entities $e \in E$ using a scoring function $s(m, e)$. If $\forall e \in E, s(m, e) < 0$ then m is added to the set E as a new entity. Otherwise, m is said to belong to the entity representation with the highest score $e^* = \text{argmax}_{e \in E}\ s(m, e)$ and the representation of e^* is updated to be the mean of all mention representations that the entity represents thus far. This method is referred to as the Unbounded Memory (U-MEM) model in the original work.

For training we use the default hyperparameters except for those that are specific to the pretrained encoder or number of training steps. We use the default optimizer of AdamW with a learning rate of 1e-5 for the pretrained encoder and 3e-4 for all other parameters.

Mention Heads The shared task evaluation requires the annotation of mention heads for each mention. We estimate mention heads from the provided dependency tree using heuristics provided by the Udapi library (Popel et al., 2017). Specifically, we use the command '`udapy -s corefud.MoveHead`'.

3.1 Preprocessing

We first convert the CoNLL-U files to a standardized JSON format using the file reader available in the Udapi Python library (Popel et al., 2017). We then tokenize each word independently using the pretrained encoder's tokenizer as implemented in Huggingface Transformers (Wolf et al., 2020). Finally, we concatenate all tokens together to produce a sequence of tokens representing the document.

Speaker Information We extract speaker information for each sentence from the sentence headers in the original CoNLL-U file. For example, the `CorefUD_English-GUM` corpora includes headers of the form "# speaker = <SPEAKER_NAME>" for certain documents. We include each speaker name s in the input at the beginning of the respective sentence. The name is formatted as "<speaker> s </speaker>" where <speaker> and </speaker> are randomly initialized tokens added to the model vocabulary. Including speakers as part of the text input such as in our approach was originally proposed by Wu et al. (2020).

Language Embedding We represent each language by a latent vector which is concatenated to the input of the entity-mention scoring function $s(m, e)$. The shared task datasets include 12 unique languages, so we define 12 such vectors. These language features are analogous to the OntoNotes genre features originally proposed by Wiseman et al. (2016).

Zero-anaphora When zeros appear in input (i.e., omitted pronouns that have been reconstructed in the coreference dataset), we represent these zeros as the underscore character '_' at training and test time since this is how they are represented in the CoNLL-U format.

3.2 Pretrained Encoder

We experimented with two pretrained encoders: XLM-RoBERTa (XLM-R; Conneau et al. 2020) and MT5 (Xue et al., 2021). To encode the document represented as a sequence of tokens, we split the sequence into chunks of maximum length L, encode the chunks using the pretrained encoder, and then concatenate the token encodings. Based on the sequence lengths the models were originally pretrained with, we use $L = 512$ for XLM-R and $L = 1024$ for MT5. We test using both the base and large model sizes for each encoder, up to 559M parameters for XLM-R and 995M parameters for MT5. In future work, it might be interesting to test RemBERT (Chung et al., 2021) as well, which was found by Straka and Straková (2022) to outperform XLM-R for multilingual coreference resolution.

3.3 Joint Training

We experiment with three methods for jointly training the model on all datasets: 1) **uniform weighting** where all datasets are sampled from equally; 2) **proportional weighting** where datasets are sampled proportional to the number of training examples in the dataset; and 3) **maximum weighting** where datasets are sampled from proportional to their training set size, except that training sets over some maximum threshold size are treated as if they are of that maximum size. This amounts to downscaling larger datasets to a maximum size. In our experiments we use 500 training examples as the maximum threshold.

4 Results

In this section we first present the results experimenting with each design decision, and then present the final submission performance. In preliminary experiments, we micro-average CoNLL F1 scores across all datasets for simplicity. For the final evaluation, CoNLL F1 scores are macro-averaged across datasets.

4.1 Pretrained Encoder

We experiment with both XLM-R and MT5 at the base and large model sizes. For these experiments, we report micro-averaged, exact-match CoNLL F1

Model		CoNLL F1
XLM-R	Base	71.9
	Large	**74.4**
MT5	Base	70.3
	Large	71.5

Table 1: Effects of the pre-trained encoder. CoNLL F1 score micro-averaged across all development sets.

Sample Weighting	CoNLL F1
Uniform	70.8
Proportional	71.9
Maximum	**72.9**

Table 2: Effects of the joint training method using the XLM-R base encoder. CoNLL F1 score micro-averaged across all development sets.

on the development set (Table 1). We find that XLM-R, despite having fewer parameters and a shorter sequence length than MT5 outperforms the MT5 model. Possible explanations might be that: 1) MT5 was trained as an encoder-decoder model, while we use only the encoder for these experiments which creates a pretraining versus finetuning disparity that could hurt performance; or, 2) we finetuned the models with FP16 mixed precision whereas MT5 was pretrained with BF16 mixed precision.

4.2 Joint Training

Next, we experiment with the three methods of joint training. For this experiment we use the XLM-R base encoder. We again evaluate using exact-match CoNLL F1 micro-averaged on the development set (Table 2). We find that the maximum weighting sampling method outperformed proportional sampling in this evaluation. For our final submission, we use a model first trained with proportional weighting for 50 epochs and next trained with maximum weighting for 50 epochs using early stopping on the development set.

4.3 Final Submission

Our final model achieves 65.43 F1 on the test set and fourth place in the competition (Table 3). We see a relatively high variance of the model ranking across languages (Table 4): for example, achieving second place on German-PotsdamCC and yet seventh place on both Czech-PDT and German-ParCorFull. This seems to be correlated with the relative size of the datasets, German-PotsdamCC being much larger than German-ParCorFull. Better performance on low-resource datasets is therefore a possible way to improve the performance of multilingual, entity-ranking models.

system	head-match	partial-match	exact-match	with singletons
1. CorPipe	74.90	73.33	71.46	76.82
2. Anonymous	70.41	69.23	67.09	73.20
3. Ondfa	69.19	68.93	53.01	68.37
4. **McGill**	65.43	64.56	63.13	68.23
5. DeepBlueAI	62.29	61.32	59.95	54.51
6. DFKI-Adapt	61.86	60.83	59.18	53.94
7. ITUNLP	59.53	58.49	56.89	52.07
8. BASELINE	56.96	56.28	54.75	49.32
9. DFKI-MPrompt	53.76	51.62	50.42	46.83

Table 3: Final F1 scores of all submissions. McGill (bolded) refers to our final submission which achieves fourth place in all categories except exact-match, for which it is in third place.

	ca	cs_1	cs_2	de_1	de_2	en_1	en_2	es	fr	hu	lt	pl	ru	hu	no_1	no_2	tr
Baseline	65.26	67.72	65.22	44.11	57.13	63.08	35.19	66.93	55.31	55.32	63.57	66.08	69.03	40.71	65.10	65.78	22.75
McGill	71.75	67.67	70.88	41.58	70.20	66.72	47.27	73.78	65.17	65.93	65.77	76.14	77.28	60.74	73.73	72.43	45.28
Δ	6.49	-0.05	5.66	-2.53	13.07	3.64	12.08	6.85	9.86	10.61	2.2	10.06	8.25	20.03	8.63	6.65	22.53

Table 4: Head-match CoNLL F1 scores of our final submission (McGill) as compared to the shared-task baseline for each language. $Delta$ is the difference in F1 score of both models. The datasets for each language, from left to right, are: ca_ancora, cs_pcedt, cs_pdt, de_parcorfull, de_potsdamcc, en_gum, en_parcorfull, es_ancora, fr_democrat, hu_szegedkoref, lt_lcc, pl_pcc, ru_rucor, hu_korkor, no_bokmaalnarc, no_nynorsknarc, and tr_itcc.

5 Conclusion

We adapt an entity-ranking coreference resolution model to multilingual coreference resolution for the CRAC 2023 shared task. We explore the method of training and joint encoder, finally using XLM-R large and a rescaled dataset weighting in our submission. This method achieved fourth place of nine submissions in the shared task.

Acknowledgements

The authors acknowledge the material support of NVIDIA in the form of computational resources. Ian Porada is supported by a fellowship from the Fonds de recherche du Québec (FRQ). Jackie Chi Kit Cheung is supported by the Canada CIFAR AI Chair program.

References

Hyung Won Chung, Thibault Fevry, Henry Tsai, Melvin Johnson, and Sebastian Ruder. 2021. Rethinking embedding coupling in pre-trained language models. In *International Conference on Learning Representations*.

Alexis Conneau, Kartikay Khandelwal, Naman Goyal, Vishrav Chaudhary, Guillaume Wenzek, Francisco Guzmán, Edouard Grave, Myle Ott, Luke Zettlemoyer, and Veselin Stoyanov. 2020. Unsupervised cross-lingual representation learning at scale. In *Proceedings of the 58th Annual Meeting of the Association for Computational Linguistics*, pages 8440–8451, Online. Association for Computational Linguistics.

Mandar Joshi, Omer Levy, Luke Zettlemoyer, and Daniel Weld. 2019. BERT for coreference resolution: Baselines and analysis. In *Proceedings of the 2019 Conference on Empirical Methods in Natural Language Processing and the 9th International Joint Conference on Natural Language Processing (EMNLP-IJCNLP)*, pages 5803–5808, Hong Kong, China. Association for Computational Linguistics.

Kenton Lee, Luheng He, Mike Lewis, and Luke Zettlemoyer. 2017. End-to-end neural coreference resolution. In *Proceedings of the 2017 Conference on Empirical Methods in Natural Language Processing*, pages 188–197, Copenhagen, Denmark. Association for Computational Linguistics.

Michal Novák, Martin Popel, Zdeněk Žabokrtský, Daniel Zeman, Anna Nedoluzhko, Kutay Acar, Peter Bourgonje, Silvie Cinková, Gülşen Cebiroğlu Eryiğit, Jan Hajič, Christian Hardmeier, Dag Haug, Tollef Jørgensen, Andre Kåsen, Pauline Krielke, Frédéric Landragin, Ekaterina Lapshinova-Koltunski, Petter Mæhlum, M.Antònia Martí, Marie Mikulová, Anders Nøklestad, Maciej Ogrodniczuk, Lilja Øvrelid, Tuğba Pamay Arslan, Marta Recasens, Per Erik Solberg, Manfred Stede, Milan Straka, Svetlana Toldova, Noémi Vadász, Erik Velldal, Veronika Vincze, Amir Zeldes, and Voldemaras Žitkus. 2022. Coreference in universal dependencies 1.1 (CorefUD 1.1).

LINDAT/CLARIAH-CZ digital library at the Institute of Formal and Applied Linguistics (ÚFAL), Faculty of Mathematics and Physics, Charles University.

Martin Popel, Zdeněk Žabokrtský, and Martin Vojtek. 2017. Udapi: Universal API for Universal Dependencies. In *Proceedings of the NoDaLiDa 2017 Workshop on Universal Dependencies (UDW 2017)*, pages 96–101, Gothenburg, Sweden. Association for Computational Linguistics.

Ian Porada, Alexandra Olteanu, Kaheer Suleman, Adam Trischler, and Jackie Chi Kit Cheung. 2023. Investigating failures to generalize for coreference resolution models.

Sameer Pradhan, Alessandro Moschitti, Nianwen Xue, Olga Uryupina, and Yuchen Zhang. 2012. CoNLL-2012 shared task: Modeling multilingual unrestricted coreference in OntoNotes. In *Joint Conference on EMNLP and CoNLL - Shared Task*, pages 1–40, Jeju Island, Korea. Association for Computational Linguistics.

Sameer Pradhan, Lance Ramshaw, Mitchell Marcus, Martha Palmer, Ralph Weischedel, and Nianwen Xue. 2011. CoNLL-2011 shared task: Modeling unrestricted coreference in OntoNotes. In *Proceedings of the Fifteenth Conference on Computational Natural Language Learning: Shared Task*, pages 1–27, Portland, Oregon, USA. Association for Computational Linguistics.

Ondřej Pražák and Miloslav Konopík. 2022. End-to-end multilingual coreference resolution with mention head prediction. In *Proceedings of the CRAC 2022 Shared Task on Multilingual Coreference Resolution*, pages 23–27, Gyeongju, Republic of Korea. Association for Computational Linguistics.

Milan Straka and Jana Straková. 2022. ÚFAL CorPipe at CRAC 2022: Effectivity of multilingual models for coreference resolution. In *Proceedings of the CRAC 2022 Shared Task on Multilingual Coreference Resolution*, pages 28–37, Gyeongju, Republic of Korea. Association for Computational Linguistics.

Shubham Toshniwal, Sam Wiseman, Allyson Ettinger, Karen Livescu, and Kevin Gimpel. 2020. Learning to Ignore: Long Document Coreference with Bounded Memory Neural Networks. In *Proceedings of the 2020 Conference on Empirical Methods in Natural Language Processing (EMNLP)*, pages 8519–8526, Online. Association for Computational Linguistics.

Shubham Toshniwal, Patrick Xia, Sam Wiseman, Karen Livescu, and Kevin Gimpel. 2021. On generalization in coreference resolution. In *Proceedings of the Fourth Workshop on Computational Models of Reference, Anaphora and Coreference*, pages 111–120, Punta Cana, Dominican Republic. Association for Computational Linguistics.

Kellie Webster, Marta R. Costa-jussà, Christian Hardmeier, and Will Radford, editors. 2019. *GAP Shared Task Overview*.

Kellie Webster, Marta Recasens, Vera Axelrod, and Jason Baldridge. 2018. Mind the GAP: A balanced corpus of gendered ambiguous pronouns. *Transactions of the Association for Computational Linguistics*, 6:605–617.

Sam Wiseman, Alexander M. Rush, and Stuart M. Shieber. 2016. Learning global features for coreference resolution. In *Proceedings of the 2016 Conference of the North American Chapter of the Association for Computational Linguistics: Human Language Technologies*, pages 994–1004, San Diego, California. Association for Computational Linguistics.

Thomas Wolf, Lysandre Debut, Victor Sanh, Julien Chaumond, Clement Delangue, Anthony Moi, Pierric Cistac, Tim Rault, Remi Louf, Morgan Funtowicz, Joe Davison, Sam Shleifer, Patrick von Platen, Clara Ma, Yacine Jernite, Julien Plu, Canwen Xu, Teven Le Scao, Sylvain Gugger, Mariama Drame, Quentin Lhoest, and Alexander Rush. 2020. Transformers: State-of-the-art natural language processing. In *Proceedings of the 2020 Conference on Empirical Methods in Natural Language Processing: System Demonstrations*, pages 38–45, Online. Association for Computational Linguistics.

Wei Wu, Fei Wang, Arianna Yuan, Fei Wu, and Jiwei Li. 2020. CorefQA: Coreference resolution as query-based span prediction. In *Proceedings of the 58th Annual Meeting of the Association for Computational Linguistics*, pages 6953–6963, Online. Association for Computational Linguistics.

Patrick Xia, João Sedoc, and Benjamin Van Durme. 2020. Incremental neural coreference resolution in constant memory. In *Proceedings of the 2020 Conference on Empirical Methods in Natural Language Processing (EMNLP)*, pages 8617–8624, Online. Association for Computational Linguistics.

Patrick Xia and Benjamin Van Durme. 2021. Moving on from OntoNotes: Coreference resolution model transfer. In *Proceedings of the 2021 Conference on Empirical Methods in Natural Language Processing*, pages 5241–5256, Online and Punta Cana, Dominican Republic. Association for Computational Linguistics.

Linting Xue, Noah Constant, Adam Roberts, Mihir Kale, Rami Al-Rfou, Aditya Siddhant, Aditya Barua, and Colin Raffel. 2021. mT5: A massively multilingual pre-trained text-to-text transformer. In *Proceedings of the 2021 Conference of the North American Chapter of the Association for Computational Linguistics: Human Language Technologies*, pages 483–498, Online. Association for Computational Linguistics.

Zdeněk Žabokrtský, Miloslav Konopík, Anna Nedoluzhko, Michal Novák, Maciej Ogrodniczuk, Martin Popel, Ondřej Pražák, Jakub Sido, and Daniel Zeman. 2023. Findings of the Second Shared Task on Multilingual Coreference Resolution. In *Proceedings of the CRAC 2023 Shared Task on Multilingual Coreference Resolution*, pages 1–18, Singapore. Association for Computational Linguistics.

Zdeněk Žabokrtský, Miloslav Konopík, Anna Nedoluzhko, Michal Novák, Maciej Ogrodniczuk, Martin Popel, Ondřej Pražák, Jakub Sido, Daniel Zeman, and Yilun Zhu. 2022. Findings of the shared task on multilingual coreference resolution. In *Proceedings of the CRAC 2022 Shared Task on Multilingual Coreference Resolution*, pages 1–17, Gyeongju, Republic of Korea. Association for Computational Linguistics.

Author Index

Association for Computational Linguistics
209 N. Eighth Street
Stroudsburg, Pennsylvania 18360

ISBN 978-1-7138-8599-3

CURRAN ASSOCIATES INC.
proceedings.com